Praise for *Learn More Now*

"Leaders at all levels will benefit from Marcia Conner's amazing book of strategies, exercises, and stories to maximize learning. When the excitement of learning permeates organizations, people feel valued, talented, and fulfilled. This book is a must for your reading list this year."

—Ken Blanchard, Chief Spiritual Officer, Ken Blanchard Companies

"We learn so naturally as children; everything we do is about learning. As we mature, many of us lose touch with this innate approach to learning. Marcia Conner's book provides a roadmap to reawakening the natural process of integrating learning into our daily lives."

—Kathy O'Driscoll, Human Resources Director, Microsoft

"*Learn More Now* combines ease and simplicity with surprising depth. It's easy to learn what Conner is saying, yet her insights are remarkably deep, allowing for some major shifts in approach. *Learn More Now* makes learning—from books or work or conferences or family or life itself—richer, deeper, and, best of all, both fun and easy. Conner made me see old things in new ways, offering simple tactics to make lots of gains in learning. With the tremendous pace of life, *Learn More Now* is like a twenty-point tune-up that improves the efficiency of the most important tool we have—our minds."

—Daniel Granholm Mulhern, Leadership Consultant
and First Gentleman of the State of Michigan

"*Learn More Now* is a very practical, hands-on resource that has enabled me to develop a much better understanding of how I obtain knowledge and skill and has provided me with best practices for dealing with individuals of differing approaches. The content of the book is very insightful and includes great workbook-style exerci~~ ~~ ~~t~~ facilitate learning by doing. *Learn More Now* coaches individuals to ~~~~~~~~~~~ness and provides tips and techniques for buildi~~ ~~ ~~~~nt to individual and business success. *Lea* ~~~~~~~, and filled with wonderful quotes that pr ~~~~~~ plication of what I've learned through rea~~ ~~ ovide me with a repeatable, successful process for future grow~~ ~~ ~~elopment."

—Karen Kocher, Vice President of CIGNA Technology Institute, CIGNA

"*Learn More Now* is a treat for everybody interested in learning smarter. Finally, a publication that genuinely respects learner diversity as much as it offers tangible ideas for dealing with it. Marcia L. Conner is a true learning champion. In *Learn More Now* she walks the talk by sharing her immense knowledge about her vocation in a language that resonates with learning specialists as much as novices in that field. *Learn More Now* presents the complexity of human learning in simple language. Trust the author, take her advice, stay with her to give your learning journey the boost you deserve.

"Learning can be a challenging task; talking to clients in the past, I have always emphasized that there is no shortcut to learning. *Learn More Now* proves me wrong. *Learn More Now* will become an indispensable companion on my own learning journey."

—Gunnar Brückner, former Chief Learning Officer,
United Nations Development Programme

Learn More Now

10 Simple Steps
to Learning
Better, Smarter,
and Faster

MARCIA L. CONNER

WILEY

John Wiley & Sons, Inc.

Published by John Wiley & Sons, Inc., Hoboken, New Jersey
Published simultaneously in Canada

Illustrations by Kavita Bali, Urban Peacock (www.urbanpeacock.com)

Design and production by Navta Associates, Inc.

For general information about our other products and services, please contact our Customer Care Department within the United States at (800) 762-2974, outside the United States at (317) 572-3993 or fax (317) 572-4002.

Wiley also publishes its books in a variety of electronic formats. Some content that appears in print may not be available in electronic books. For more information about Wiley products, visit our web site at www.wiley.com.

Library of Congress Cataloging-in-Publication Data:
Conner, Marcia L., date.
     Learn more now : 10 simple steps to learning better, smarter, and faster / Marcia L. Conner
       p.   cm.
Includes bibliographical references and index.
     ISBN 0-471-27390-2 (pbk.)
1. Learning. 2. Cognitive styles. I. Title.
LB1060.C655 2004
370.15'23—dc22
                                                                                2003017819

Printed in the United States of America
10 9 8 7 6 5

This book is dedicated to the memory of
Douglas C. McBride (1952–1996)

Contents

Acknowledgments

The path I followed to write this book seems similar to the route we each face when embarking on any big journey—apprehension, wonder, curiosity, attention, exhaustion, and eventually joy when we can recognize our learning and everyone who illuminated our way.

My heartfelt thanks to the people who directly and indirectly, personally and professionally, introduced me to timeless ideas, spurred on original thinking, generously told me what they really thought, and created a space for me to flourish. I am especially indebted to those who sent a steady stream of love and belonging no matter how isolated I became doing the years I devoted to this work.

Specifically, Brenda Wilkins tenderly asked the right questions. David MacKenzie brought forth an underlying energy. Ellen Wagner tenaciously reminded me to clear my meanings. Gretchen Lee introduced a way to say what I felt. Susan McGinnis elegantly evoked associations as she read the full manuscript.

Kellee Sikes, Joel Getzendanner, Judee Humburg, David Grebow, and Bill Owen equilibrated my perceptions early and often. Martha Spruitenburg, Clark Quinn, Joann Ward, Gunnar Brückner, Alan Zametkin, Ken Kousky, John Kirkham, Dean Alms, and Vicki Halsey drew me toward grand concepts beyond my horizon.

Jimm Meloy, Rich Persaud, Brook Manville, Estee Solomon Gray, John Seely Brown, Michael Carter, Eric Vogt, Tom Hill, Verna Allee, Eilif Trondsen, Dave Forman, Elliott Masie, Tom Hurley, Rob Harris, Mike Savage, Jack Morris, Kirk Fleming, Ron Shevlin, Susan Bernstein, and Marc Rosenberg dared me to look from emergent directions. Bob Bruner, Debbie Fisher, and my colleagues at the Darden School's Batten Institute offered pivotal advice at precisely the right moments.

Susan Rundle, Rita Dunn, Bob Filipczak, Michael Dertouzos, John

Ratey, Richard Eyre, and Sandra Conn, through their writings and a few priceless conversations, challenged me to offer fresh perspectives.

Debra Young, Beth Garlington Scofield, Melinda Lee, Kelly Mecham, Will Luckert, Elizabeth O'Halloran, Plum Cluverius, Leanne Gallagher, Ginger Sall, Steve Tennant, Marjorie Pingel, Kathy O'Driscoll, and Jim Clawson gracefully cared for my inner self. Susan McNaughton, Jodi Sheinis, Polly Slater, Denise LaRue, Julie Ray, Cami Smith, Ann Betts, Jeanne Schmidt, Alicia Vause, Alan Van Winkle, Shelly Sweet, Sandra MacKenzie, Lisa Nichols, Mark Cavender, David Goldsmith, and Todd Greenstein had miraculous faith in me.

Jay Cross, Barb Stuart, Rhonda Rosenof, Hal Richman, Allison Scott Majure, Sandy Vilas, Vince Wilk, Toni Boyle, Damian Zakakis, Bill Cumming, Kevin Bruny, Cheryl Emory, Greg Roberts, and the LLLI review network cheered me on like guardian angels.

Harlan Cleveland, Doug Englebart, Michael Schrage, Elizabeth Teisberg, Charlotte Lobe, Carmen Zeider, and Shirley McArdle serve as role models and sources of ongoing inspirations.

Amy Halliday, Ann Longknife, and Maya Porter showed me how to simultaneously unravel and tighten my words so that you can follow along. Kantha Shelke nurtured the final chapter with aplomb.

My parents, Ann and Bob, taught me how to be brave during unbearably difficult times and modeled for me lifelong learning. My in-laws, Jo Ann and Charlie, lovingly took large responsibilities off my shoulders and helped me feel truly at home.

Jim Levine saw the potential and courageously pursued finding these words the right home. Tom Miller at John Wiley and Sons inspired me to get down to the examples, overcome obscurity, and say what I mean. Hope Breeman patiently kept me on schedule and had a gift for answering my endless questions.

The notion that I could write a book grew from a potent conversation with two extraordinary gentlemen, Wayne Hodgins and Doug McBride, almost a decade ago. Without their compelling vision and their unwavering commitment to learning, I might not have ever stopped to write any of this down. I am stronger because Wayne continues to be an attentive friend, an uncompromising critic, and a loving cheerleader.

One night my husband, Karl, listening to me give myself a hard time over the wording of a sentence, whispered, "Be gentle with my wife, this book is her baby." If that's so, he helped bring her into the world. During the gestation, he built a house for us to live in, endured months of driving to and from airports, and persistently straightened out what really mattered. Without his tender and insightful understanding, this book would not exist.

Finally, I am grateful to the hundreds of people who have helped light my passageway. Although many names are mentioned in these chapters, I couldn't include stories from all of the learners who over the years recounted for me their adventures. I am indebted to everyone who has ever taken the time to help clarify my message by introducing me to their personal style.

Learn More Now

Introduction

The day I came home from camp, the summer between third and fourth grades, my five-year-old brother swam the length of our neighborhood swimming pool, climbed into my mother's arms, and died. This sudden, tragic, and unexpected event changed all of our lives forever.

That fall, my fourth-grade teacher, sensing my impatience with schoolwork, suggested that I learn to think like a teacher instead of a student. Before she taught each lesson, she showed me the techniques and strategies she would use with our class. With warm words and creative counsel, she instilled in me a love of learning.

You might expect me to say that this also infused me with an appreciation for schooling, but it didn't. I had an eerie insight that my needs were different from my classmates'. After all, my experiences were different from theirs; what I thought about was different, and what I learned—and how I learned it—was different as well.

I became even more uncomfortable when I realized that I wasn't the only *different* one. My classmates also had exceptional experiences and needs. For instance, my friend Julie's parents had recently gone through a difficult divorce. Steve had gained ten pounds over the summer. Beth's family moved away from the only neighborhood she'd ever known.

We needed more from our teacher than a handful of cookie-cutter instructional methods and the curriculum she was required to teach. We needed personalization. Instead of feeling inspired to become a school teacher (which might have been a terrific profession for me), at age nine I became suspicious of anyone or anything that didn't honor people's differences. My teacher delivered the same message, in the same way, at the same time to every student, expecting the same result. I felt alienated and discouraged.

What turned me around was the ongoing encouragement from my parents, who filled me with aphorisms from Friedrich Nietzsche and Albert Einstein, such as, "If you can live through this, you can live through anything," and "We can't solve problems by using the same kind of thinking we used when we created them." They urged me to use my unbounded energy to figure out a better way.

I appreciate what my fourth-grade teacher offered because she helped me develop a cause, a passion, and a drive. Since that time, I've thought about, tried out, challenged, and learned from learning nearly every day. My goal hasn't been to learn more but to get more from the life I live—and to help others become the curious, wide-eyed learners they once were.

When I attempted to graduate from college, I faced a new challenge. I was labeled as having a learning disability, for which I had compensated since childhood. Without knowing it, I had developed a string of alternative learning methods. For the first time, I realized that some of my aggravation with school wasn't only from dealing with the distraction of my brother's death. I was actually unable to pay attention in the way my classmates could. This unexpected turn gave me a chance to spend time with brain researchers at the National Institutes of Mental Health who used positron-emission tomography (PET), a cutting-edge technology for understanding the mechanics of how people learn.

Next, in a series of serendipitous events, a small publishing firm and then Microsoft hired me to make complicated ideas easier to understand. (In those days, what Microsoft did was so enigmatic that my mother thought I had gone to work for a very soft toilet paper manufacturer.) Microsoft was the first place where I didn't feel different or alone. Everyone in the technology sector seemed different—very energetic and looking for innovative solutions.

Since then, I've worked with all sorts of organizations—from corporations and governments to associations and schools—all over the world. With each one, I help figure out how to move the focus of learning from one department to every department, and I help people learn not only in their offices but at home and in their communities.

To do this, I explored everything that I could in the field of learning. I delighted in unearthing historic answers from the education field that I'd never seen put into use in the workplace. I encountered extraordinary scientists working on breakthrough theories that hadn't yet reached mainstream publications. I reflected on fantastic discoveries about my own human operating system, which seem to resonate with people who also suspect that there's a better way.

One day after I gave a presentation on how learning influences every aspect of life, the man sitting beside me introduced himself as a literary agent. He asked me to consider writing a book about how we learn across the life span, a book that didn't neglect modern themes, including information overload, personal and professional relationships, paying attention in chaotic times, the role of the learner's environment, and even learning to just be. At his urging, I began to condense, de-jargon, compile, and put into practical terms the keys to learn more now.

I'm not an educational theorist or a professional writer. I'm a practitioner who spends my days learning, teaching, coaching, and learning some more. I share my personal experiences and explain an approach that's based on years of experience with thousands of people in a wide variety of settings. I've also put the concepts and theories of scientists and academics, usually written in their own jargon, into actionable and embraceable suggestions you can use right away.

This book is part road map, part blueprint, and part magical decoder ring, all rolled into one. The primary purpose of this book is to help you create a meaningful and fulfilling life by embracing the nature of continual learning. It's also about more than just learning. *Learn More Now* will help you become more aware, more focused, aligned with your natural pace, and improvisational in whatever you do. It will encourage you to learn your own life's lessons, and grow into your potential.

Because some readers want to read the nitty-gritty behind these steps, I've loaded my web site (www.marciaconner.com) with citations, statistics, and additional reading beyond what you'll find in the resource section at the end of this book. Also on the web site are instructions for accessing this information in different modes and for joining other people around the world who are also interested in learning.

The techniques I use may seem deceptively simple. In this book, I offer them to you in the same way that I've shared them with people of all ages who were then able to learn better, smarter, and faster. These materials are a jumping-off place, a beginning, an adventure into uncharted territories. I gently challenge you to become more aware of how you learn and to further develop the innate ability that you've had all along.

In writing this book, I took into account that everyone reads and understands differently. With that in mind, be flexible with yourself as you explore. Even though the book is set up as ten steps, there are no rules for how to begin. For people who prefer to learn in a logical sequence, I organized the material in a way that builds from chapter to chapter. If you would rather look through everything first, you may want to skim the entire book and then start at a place that meets your specific needs. Alternatively, read the book over several weeks or even months. Or maybe you'd enjoy setting aside a few hours each week to work through the book, practicing each technique before moving on to the next chapter. If, at any point, you find that what you're reading is irrelevant to your life, jump around or skip entire sections. As you learn about yourself, you can adjust how you work with the materials, as well as your own style and pace.

When you begin to realize how you learn, how you make sense of your surroundings, and how you respond to new information, you'll naturally adjust your situation. From there, you can go deeper, learning as much or as little as you want along the way. Ready?

1

Find Your Motivation

We are not what we know but what we are willing to learn.
—*Mary Catherine Bateson*

I have great expectations of you, but none higher than you may attain.
—*Thomas Jefferson*

I n school, if there were such a category, I could have been voted, "Most likely to succeed if only she can figure herself out." My teachers' focus on class schedules and subjects, rather than on discovering and experiencing, left me feeling overwhelmed and fearing that I wasn't motivated to learn. Years later I began a journey of self-discovery, where I found that learning how to learn was my road map to success and that inside each of us is a curious learner, naturally motivated to learn more. Learning about learning can help you understand your family, friends, coworkers, and customers and, most of all, yourself.

This book reveals techniques and conditions to help you learn how to learn about whatever interests you. My focus isn't on the content of learning but, rather, on the process of learning itself. You might choose to pursue a personally relevant topic or a subject that other people have suggested would improve your life. When you focus on how you learn, you can decide which techniques work best and reflect on how you've successfully learned things in the past.

The motivation inventory in this chapter provides an opportunity for you to discover what drives you to learn and what might hold you back. Then you can decide how to adjust your circumstances to address your needs. Once you know your own motivations and can better understand those of the people around you, you can improve almost anything you do.

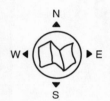

Road Map to This Chapter

Chapter 1 takes you to the following destinations:

▶ Learning what motivates you to learn

▶ Setting goals

▶ Seeking opportunities

▶ Teaching someone what you learn

▶ Keeping a journal

▶ Overcoming anxiety

Preview What's Ahead

Throughout this book, you'll find small road map sections. When you begin to learn something new, a preview helps you understand the lay of the land. If you haven't skimmed the rest of this book, I encourage you to take a few minutes to do that now. Just like Lewis and Clark, we make the journey in order to create the map. Giving yourself a preview also helps you to anticipate what's next.

You can also supplement the index. When you see topics you want to return to, highlight their pages and add them, in your own words, along with their page numbers, to the index. Use sticky notes to mark the topics you want to reference quickly. Create lists in the margins, rewrite what I've written in your own words, and, please, draw pictures in the blank spaces provided. Make this your book by engaging with the materials.

Note: If this is a library book, please be considerate of future readers by keeping your notes and assessment totals on a separate sheet of paper or writing so lightly in pencil that you can erase your marks after you tally your scores.

Master Motivation

> Learning isn't about being smart enough, it is about being motivated enough.
>
> —*Marilyn Ferguson*

> Ultimately, all motivation is self-motivation. You may be offered attractive incentives, but, at best, they will only help you to decide to motivate yourself. No matter what external incentives and inducements are held out to you, you are the only person who can motivate you. This is because motivation springs from within.
>
> —*Peter Honey*

Motivation is the force that draws you to move toward something. It can come from a desire or a curiosity within you or can be from an external force urging you on. In either case, *you* make the decision to seize or to skip a chance to learn.

When learning seems interesting, fun, meaningful, or relevant, you don't have any reason to try to understand your motivation. Learning comes naturally. The challenge comes when you aspire to learn something that's not particularly interesting, when you have only a few choices, or when you lack adequate support, respect, or encouragement. In those situations, learning and finding the motivation to learn more can be tough. It's easy to think you just lack motivation.

That's not really possible, though. We're all equally motivated and we're always fully motivated. With the exception of involuntary anatomical processes, such as your heart beating, your blood flowing, or breathing in and out, everything else we do is motivated.

If you stopped reading this book now, it would be inaccurate for me to say, "You're not motivated!" For some reason, you're motivated to stop reading. That motivation was stronger than your motivation to continue.

The same could be said when you're trying to learn something from your wife, a colleague, a teacher, or a parent and you keep thinking about dinner or what to watch tonight on TV. It isn't that you're unmotivated to learn—you're just not motivated to do what someone else wants you to do at that moment. Something else is drawing you (motivating you) to focus on dinner or the TV.

It could also be that you're motivated to avoid the aggravation you feel when someone seems to be wasting your time or you have a gnawing suspicion that you will never understand something. You don't lack motivation; you lack confidence in success—and that drives your motivation elsewhere, to avoid the feeling or the fear. It's not that you were unmotivated. You were probably super-motivated. Consider how much motivation it takes to ignore something right in front of you!

Are you ready to find out what motivates you to learn? Motivation styles vary for different situations and topics, but you rely on one primarily. Some people learn in order to achieve a certain goal. Some people learn for the sake of learning, and other people learn for the gratification they get from meeting people in learning settings.

At other times, you might like being part of a group, even if your primary style is learning-motivated. Likewise, you might go wholeheartedly after a goal, even if your primary style is relationship-motivated. Many of us have learned how to be goal-motivated because our society places a premium on meeting goals.

Whether you're goal-motivated, learning-motivated, or relationship-motivated, it's helpful to recognize your predominant motivational style so that you can identify the situations that best satisfy your needs.

What's Your Motivation Style?

Take a few minutes to complete the following questionnaire assessing your preferred motivation style. Begin by reading the words in the left-hand column. Of the three responses to the right, circle the one that best characterizes you, answering as honestly as possible with the description that applies to you right now. Count the number of circled items, and write your total at the bottom of each column. These questions have no right or wrong answers. Your response offers insight about how you're motivated to learn.

1. I'm proud when I . . .	✓Get things done.	Help other people.	Think things through.
2. I mostly think about . . .	✓What's next.	People.	Ideas.
3. To relax, I tend to . . .	Do whatever it takes to accomplish relaxation.	✓Hang out and talk with friends.	Read, surf the web to learn new things.
4. I like to do things . . .	Now or on a schedule.	When it works for everyone.	✓When it feels right to me.
5. When online, I like to . . .	✓Search and retrieve.	Write e-mails, instant messages, or chat.	Look around and linger.
6. Projects should be . . .	Finished on time.	Done in groups.	✓Meaningful to me.
7. In school, I liked to . . .	Ask constant questions.	✓Make friends.	Explore.
8. Schedules . . .	Keep order.	Help coordinate people.	✓Are a useful tool.
9. I like to be recognized for . . .	Being organized, neat, productive, efficient, and punctual.	Noticing other people, being kind, fair, thoughtful, and considerate.	✓Being clever and smart, making discoveries, and solving problems.
10. In terms of completing things . . .	I finish what I start.	✓I like to enlist the help of other people.	I believe that life is a journey, not a destination.
Total	**Goal** _3_	**Relationship** _3_	**Learning** _4_

The column with the highest total represents your primary motivation style. The column with the second-highest total is your secondary motivation style.

My primary motivation style: _____Learning_____

My secondary motivation style: _____Goal / Relational_____

If you're goal-motivated, you probably reach for your goals through a direct and obvious route. This might lead you to a reference book, to a computer, or to call an expert—whatever means is available. You usually prefer meeting in person only when it's the most effective method to get what you need, and you probably don't find learning, in and of itself, much fun.

If you're relationship-motivated, you learn mainly for social contact. When you meet and interact with people, you learn things at the same time. You may not like working independently or focusing on topics (separately from people) because that doesn't give you the interaction you crave.

If you're learning-motivated, the practice of learning, itself, compels you. You seek out knowledge for its own sake and may become frustrated by anything that requires you to spend more time on procedure and process than on actual learning.

There is also a fourth motivation style that I haven't addressed, primarily because it's less common than the other three and because you might not think of it as a motivation style at all. That style is thrill-motivated, drawn not to any particular thing but, rather, away from anything that people perceive as tying them down, bounding them, or pulling them in any predictable direction. This isn't to say that thrill-motivated learners can't acquire goals, relationships, or curiosity, but if any of these feel too time-consuming, invasive, or binding, the learner becomes restless and perhaps experiences a compulsion to go in another direction—any other direction—to feel free. If you're thrill-motivated, you're likely to be impulsive and you want to remain impulsive; you seek out excitement and flee anything that doesn't offer you that sensation. All of us, at one time or another, feel impetuous, but we usually moderate these urges when they come, instead of always following where they lead.

Let's look more closely at the three predominant styles.

Are You Goal-Motivated?

If you don't know where you're going, any path will take you there.

—Sioux proverb

Goal-motivated people look at learning as a way to solve problems, pursue particular interests, and accomplish clear-cut objectives. If you're goal-motivated, you probably believe that you should use what you know. You might ask "Why else would anyone bother learning it?"

Ongoing learning for the goal-motivated comes in waves. You might realize that you need to learn something specific or you may have identified an interest that can help you excel. For instance, you might hire a coach or a trainer in a particular area so that you can get a promotion. You might read a book, go on a trip, or join a learning group to master something new. When you do spend energy on learning, you usually don't restrict your activities to any one source or method. You likely pursue whatever means necessary to reach your goal.

Goal-motivated skills are required to complete any project. School, for instance, rewards students for being goal-motivated—for turning in their assignments on time, neatly written, and properly punctuated. Accomplishing goals is perhaps the most valued and most necessary motivation in our society. Therefore, most of us develop some goal-oriented skills, whether or not that's what motivates us.

Robert, a stockbroker, is a typical goal-motivated learner, who finds useful articles related to his work on the Internet, in newspapers, in trade magazines, and in professional journals. He belongs to organizations where he can talk with people about markets and he asks everyone he meets about companies that he might want to invest in. He's constantly learning with a specific purpose. However, unless he can see how what he learns will help him achieve a goal, he isn't likely to try to learn anything new.

Wanda, a project manager, makes her living finding a balance between order and efficiency while reaching for a goal. She enjoys working with technology but doesn't think computers are very interesting. Instead, she seeks out projects that require the use of different types of technology, so she is forced to find mentors, to read manuals to inform herself, and to use her time to accomplish her goal. She also uses these projects as opportunities to coach people who are new to her type of work or who have switched careers. This gives her a fresh perspective on her old methods. She finds that the process challenges her to learn more and at a deeper level.

Tips for Goal-Motivated Learners

Here are several tips to help you reach your goals that you might not have already considered.

Take a break. We all need time to recharge our energy, even if goal-motivated people have a hard time doing so. If you think downtime is another name for "unproductive time," remind yourself that a short stretch or a five-minute walk will boost your efficiency and help you reach your goals.

Make relaxation your objective. Set a goal to do nothing for a certain amount of time each day. You'll come back to your work with a clearer head and the ability to achieve more goals.

Learn new methods. Boost your learning repertoire by setting new goals for yourself—big goals that require you to experiment with methods you haven't used before.

What Works for You?

Spend a few minutes thinking about what you find especially effective or frustrating when you try to learn. Write down what you find useful or useless so that you minimize what's aggravating and increase what's helpful when you learn in the future.

I find that the following things help me to learn.

_____

(Example: A belief that what I spend time on will help me meet my goal. Expedience. The Internet. Experts who can give a definitive answer.)

I find that the following things aggravate me when I learn.

_____

(Example: People who can't get to the point. Wasting time.)

What can I do to maximize helpful situations and minimize aggravating ones?

_____

(Example: Always begin a project by finding someone who has done it before. Find out if that person can help me. Cut out any intermediary. Talk to the source.)

Working with Goal-Motivated Learners

If you work with a goal-motivated learner, try these tips to work with that goal-driven style.

State the goals first. You can get a goal-motivated learner to see the importance of almost anything if you first clearly state a goal.

Focus on what's important. Respect that they prefer order, efficiency, and being productive by getting and staying on topic.

Find a goal, any goal. If you want a goal-motivated learner to do something that has no clearly identifiable goal for him or her, offer a goal from someone else's perspective. For instance, if you want your goal-motivated husband to take you to the movies, suggest that the goal is quality time with his spouse. Suggest that your goal-motivated sister read an article to make you happy. The goal for going out to dinner could be to avoid having to clean up the kitchen.

Recognize what makes them exceptional. Acknowledge goal-motivated learners for moving forward, for completing milestones, for wrapping things up, and for always staying focused.

 ## Are You Relationship-Motivated?

When you hug someone, you learn something else about them. An important something else.

—*E. L. Konigsburg*

Relationship-motivated learners get involved because they like the social interaction that learning offers. If you ask them why they suppose people want to learn, they may make comments like, "People learn so they have more to talk about with other people," or, "They want to meet people who care about the same things they do."

If you're a relationship-motivated person in a work-alone job, you might look for a sense of camaraderie in classes because they're socially accepted places to meet people and make friends. When a class is not available, you probably make your decisions about where to learn according to the personal relationships each opportunity offers.

If you're relationship-motivated, you might not enjoy solo activities like reading unless there is a social component such as talking about books in a reading group. Likewise, self-study learning programs probably aren't for you unless you can also interact in person or online in real time.

Carmen, a customer-support manager, and I once attended a workshop on negotiation together. It was held in a large ballroom with hundreds of other participants. I was fascinated by the compelling speaker and information that I had never encountered before. Carmen, in contrast, began talking to other people, asking them questions, and finding out how the subject related to their work. When she happened to meet another relationship-motivated learner, they moved on to unrelated topics, including families and personal interests, forging a bond based on their similar outlook, not on class material.

Matthew, a process engineer, visited the office of almost every member of our work team before beginning his own tasks, asking coworkers about their evenings, what they had planned for the week, and whether anyone wanted to get together for lunch or for an afternoon walk around the block. Although some of our coworkers thought he was avoiding his job, he needed to personally connect with each person to motivate himself to continue his often solitary quest.

Tips for Relationship-Motivated Learners

Here are a few tips to help you integrate learning and working with other people.

Find the right people to talk with. If you're relationship-motivated, you're most likely attracted to friendly people or those who want to talk through a problem. Find other people who like to build relationships and spend time with them, instead of becoming aggravated with people less interested in conversation.

Find ways to relax with other people. Spend your down-time talking on the telephone, going to social events, and meeting people.

Look out for yourself. Because you care about people, you might get sidetracked by those who want your help. Find ways to be helpful, but also reserve time and energy to develop your own social interests.

Pick your moments. To learn, you need a sense of connection with other people. Too much talking, though, can interfere with other people's styles. Find ways to work with people that honor what each of you needs.

Compare notes. If you're required to keep quiet while learning something, compare notes with other people afterward. They will understand or remember things you haven't, and vice versa.

Talk with children. Ask your children what they think of the ideas in this book. Let them tell you their feelings and experiences about learning. Ask questions such as "Which classes (or subjects) do you enjoy?" "What do you like about them?" "How can you use some of the ideas in this book?" "Is there something new you want to learn?"

You might find it motivating to think about your favorite people to learn with whenever you set out to learn something new. This exercise can help focus your attention on learning through relationships.

Name the people you work with who are relationship-motivated.

1.

2.

3.

List some times in a professional setting when it's appropriate to talk casually with people.

1.

2.

What situations are off-limits for talking with other people?

1.

2.

Observe other people who continue to learn; why do you think they do?

1.

2.

What Works for You?

Spend a few minutes reflecting on anything you find especially effective or frustrating when you try to learn. Then, write these down so that in the future, you minimize the aggravating obstacles and increase the positive experiences.

I find the following things helpful when I learn.

_____

(Example: People who are interested in talking with me. Online communities with real-time chat. Talking with my sister or my father about a subject.)

I find the following things aggravating when I learn.

_____

(Example: People who are too focused on work to talk about their experiences. Technology. Technical books.)

What can I do to maximize helpful situations and minimize aggravating ones?

_____

(Example: I need to find people I can talk with about a subject I want to learn. It could be in a class, at the library, at home, or in an office. Some of my neighbors may want to meet once a week to talk about this, too.)

Working with Relationship-Motivated Learners

If you work with relationship-motivated learners, try these tips to strengthen your relationship with them.

Help them to help other people. You can effectively work with relationship-motivated learners by recognizing their desire to contribute to the well-being of other people.

Ask for help in a supportive way. Relationship-motivated learners sometimes neglect their own families and friends because they're so busy taking care of other people. If you need their help, set time limits on your request so that you don't get in the way of their own obligations.

Put the goal in relationship terms. If you want to inspire relationship-motivated people, show them how they can build relationships while working toward your goal and how they can help other people as the project or the objective is completed.

Acknowledge what makes them special. Relationship-motivated learners are excited by a chance to talk, and they beam when given a personal note and a public acknowledgment. Praise relationship-motivated people for their kindness, fairness, thoughtfulness, and consideration.

Are You Learning-Motivated?

Education is not the filling of a pail, but the lighting of a fire.

—*William Butler Yeats*

Learning-motivated people seek knowledge because of their deep love of learning anything new. In addition to learning formally in a class or with a group, you are likely to seek out educational programs on television and the radio, read books and magazines, and take in as much information as you can. When you travel, you probably read about your destination before you go and visit every local landmark once you get there.

Many learning-motivated people have been aware of their preoccupation with learning for a long time. You may even have chosen your job or made other life decisions according to the potential for growth these opportunities offer.

Jodi, a marketing manager, developed a love of reading early in life. No one at home read much when she was growing up, but she found the library and spent as much time there as possible. Now she often reads to her daughter, hoping that this will instill a similar love of learning and reading.

Ed, a medic, always talks with his patients about their interests and hobbies, their work and their families. It helps to take their minds off their injuries or ailments and gives him an ongoing opportunity to learn all day, every day. He has as much fun learning about their photography or music as his brother gets from playing golf.

May, a social architect, has one primary measure for determining which consulting engagements to accept. She asks herself, "Does this assignment offer me an opportunity to learn something that is important to me and the world and that I couldn't easily learn anyplace else?" If it does, she accepts. If not, she encourages the client to work with someone else.

Tips for Learning-Motivated People

These tips will help you learn more about how you learn.

Share your motivation. Sometimes people can't understand why you would want to learn such diverse topics. When you explain the benefits of what you learn, though, they may support your efforts.

Write something down. If you tend to think of writing as a waste of time (because so much has already been written and is waiting to be read), consider that writing gives you an opportunity to learn from your own patterns and to recollect on what you've already learned.

Make events learning opportunities. If meetings or social gatherings seem to waste your time because they don't offer you enough to learn, try to learn something odd or unusual about each person there.

Learn from other styles. When you encounter people who are goal-motivated, ask them if you can help them find an answer.

Engage relationship-motivated people in conversation about what you've learned.

You can strengthen your motivation to learn by reflecting on what you want to learn now.

Name some things you want to learn:

1.

2.

3.

Tell a story about something you learned along the way, even though you weren't expecting it:

_____

_____

_____

_____

What Works for You?

Spend a few minutes thinking about things you find especially useful or frustrating when you try to learn more. Then write them down so that in the future you maximize whatever helps you and minimize what aggravates you.

I find the following helpful when I learn.

_____

(Example: Obtaining as much information as possible, from a rich and wide range of resources. I especially like interesting or odd details and facts.)

I find the following things aggravating when I learn.

_____

(Example: I hate it when people tell me "what's interesting," or they try to limit what I can learn more about.)

What can I do to maximize helpful situations and minimize aggravating ones?

_____

(Example: I'm not very interested in making situations learning-focused. I learn from everything. I just need to get away from people who try to control what I learn.)

Working with Learning-Motivated People

If you work with someone who is learning-motivated, try these tips to learn with them.

Offer your support. Their desire to learn won't go away. Ask yourself what you can learn from them, and what they can learn from you.

Put goals in learning terms. If you need to accomplish a goal with learning-motivated people, point out the things they'll learn along the way.

Transform parties into learning labs. When you want to entice learning-motivated people to attend a social event, suggest that they use the get-together to study social interactions and analyze how relationships work.

Answer questions. Learning-motivated people are inquisitive. Recognize that they're trying to make a connection with you through their many questions.

Try shifting the focus. Learning-motivated people can become engrossed in many subjects that interest them. If you're looking for a connection, try to draw their attention to a topic that also meets your needs.

Spotlight what makes them valuable. Take time to acknowledge learning-motivated people for being clever and innovative, for making discoveries, and solving problems.

One way to address different styles is to notice what people gain from working together. For instance, you can express to goal-motivated learners that relationship-motivated learners wouldn't likely participate without some face-to-face time and that you'll keep meetings as short as is practical. You might point out learning moments to those with a learning-motivated bent and remind relationship-motivated learners that goal- and learning-motivated people are interested in working together if the group also helps them in other ways.

You're One of a Kind

No one can be exactly like me. Sometimes even I have trouble doing it.

—*Tallulah Bankhead*

There is no "effective personality." The effective executives I have seen differ widely in their temperaments and their abilities, in what they do and in how they do it, in their personalities, their knowledge, their interests—in fact, almost everything that distinguishes human beings. All they have in common is their ability to get the right things done.

—*Peter Drucker*

Before we delve into more learning styles and preferences, let me clear up one thing you might already be thinking. No one style is better or worse than any other—just different. Each style is a part of you and a doorway to what you learn. Your actions and preferences can never be completely describable with any one style and neither will the styles of your family members or people you work with.

Because everyone is a product of both biology and experience, each person is unique and never completely predictable. The styles and preferences in this book are only characterizations. No one is just goal-motivated or learning-motivated. Yet being goal-motivated is an attribute, and knowing about motivation helps us to infer how we might approach information and be able to direct other people to position information so that it makes sense to us.

Over the years, I've found that some people become uncomfortable if they're characterized as being different. Other people seek out ways to make differentiations. This seems to be because some people tend to see similar things as being different, and other people see dissimilar things as being almost alike. How our blends of uniqueness, differences, and specialties relate to one another fascinates me, because I fit into the first category. To give an example, I'm so intrigued by our subtle differences that during a meal, I might ask someone I've just met, "Do you eat for taste or for texture?" If this type of characterizing makes you uncomfortable, you probably fit into the second group.

Motivation-Related Exercises

> Why not spend some time determining what is worthwhile
> for us, and then go after *that?*
>
> —*William Ross*

To engage your motivation and help you get the most from this book, I encourage you to work through some specific activities. Each one is short and straightforward, and you can use it to learn more about other topics, too.

Set Goals

Even if you don't identify yourself as a goal-motivated learner, you can learn from setting goals. I believe you'll benefit by spending a few minutes to identify your desired outcomes at the beginning of any book. This is also true for anything new you set out to do.

The following series of questions can help you clarify your goals and gain perspective on what you'd like to accomplish and why. Answer these questions here or on a separate piece of paper, or just ponder the answers as you work through the rest of the book.

What do you want to improve or increase, because of having read this book, and why? *My ability to Learn more & use the internet as a conduit to my Success*

List areas where you want to learn more, want better performance, or both.

1. *Management/management styles*

2. *Internet Capabilities*

3. *How to Stay on track*

Give three reasons why it's important for you to reach or exceed these goals.

1. *Be more successful Personally & Professionally*

2. *Set myself up for a good paying Job after Retirement*

3. *Reaching a long Life goal*

Today, what keeps you from reaching these goals?

1. *Everyday Job Demands*

2. *Staying motivated*

What can you do today and in the future to eliminate these obstacles?

1. *Complete task at work ahead of time*

2. *Establishing a Routine & sticking to it*

What might you lose if you don't reach your goals?
Self Satisfaction

What would change for better or worse if you do? *my Confidence Level of succeedJ at wht evn I do*

Even if you're not a goal-motivated learner, you might find it helpful to list the following five things each time you start to learn something new.

Goal: _____

(*Example: My goal is to learn how to learn more.*)

Action: _____

(*Example: I'm going to read through this book before my performance review in April.*)

Dates/Times: _____

(*Example: Set aside two hours each week during the month of March to read at least one chapter.*)

Obstacles: _____

(*Example: Busy schedule already!*)

Support: _____

(*Example: My daughter is also reading this book so we can talk about it as we go.*)

By identifying your aims, you not only see how well you accomplish them, but you also have a point of reference to work from.

Seek Opportunities

> Wherever I have knocked, a door has opened. Wherever I have wandered, a path has appeared. I have been helped, supported, encouraged, and nurtured by people of all races, creeds, colors, and dreams.
>
> —*Alice Walker*

> One must still have chaos in oneself to be able to give birth
> to a dancing star.
>
> —*Friedrich Niezsche*

Sometimes life itself educes you to learn—and it's up to you to take advantage of those opportunities. In the event that you still think of learning as only workshops or classes, expand your definition to include conversations with your peers and your children, from books, articles, informal networks, mentoring, coaching, searching on the Internet, television, movies, and even what you learn through trial and error.

Take responsibility for learning from everything. As you begin to understand how you learn you can use anything that happens in your world as a source of, and a resource for, learning more.

This matrix can help you see even more opportunities for learning. It categorizes your options into four different groups.

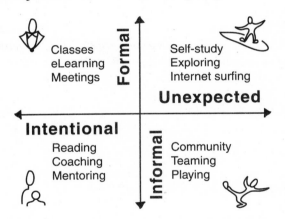

Formal intentional learning is usually structured for us. *Formal unintentional* learning happens when we seek out structured activities but are unsure what they will uncover. *Informal intentional* learning is structured by us. *Informal unexpected* learning happens in the course of everyday activities.

Begin by asking yourself what you've learned recently and in which situations your greatest learning takes place. Are you limiting your thinking to meetings or study? Have you considered seeking out a coach or a mentor, or simply finding time to explore? Might you be experiencing real learning during a walk around the block, a friendly argument with a friend, or a hard look in the mirror? Become mindful of both your formal opportunities and these types of impromptu chances to learn.

Teach Other People

> If you have knowledge, let others light their candles with it.
>
> —*Winston Churchill*

Many people tell me they are more motivated to learn when they know that they'll need to use what they've learned right away. For this reason, I encourage you to think about someone who you might teach this material to and begin to work with that person as you go through each step.

Teaching something to another person shouldn't be any more complicated than asking people you spend time with whether they would like to hear about something you learned today.

When you learn something so that you can teach it to other people, you usually learn it more completely and you focus with a different clarity than when you learn it only for yourself. You discover whether you really understand the material, and you think, "If I'm going to teach this to someone else, then I need to pay attention and think about how to explain this myself."

Introduce what you learned, highlighting what struck you as especially insightful, and then offer a little background to provide context. Ask the person you're teaching to help you learn more by offering his or her experiences and insights, asking you questions, and expanding on what you've said.

Take time now to identify someone you'll teach about motivation styles. Commit to sharing the key points from each day's material.

I will teach this to: _____

Try to apply what you learn in this book to your teaching approach. By now, you probably realize that the style that suits you best might not suit the person you're teaching. With each chapter, ask how your approach is working and how you might vary your approach so that you both can learn more.

Keep a Journal

I guess this is kind of a ratty question, but what have you written lately?

—Audrey Hepburn

If you would not be forgotten, as soon as you are dead and rotten, either write things worth reading, or do things worth the writing.

—Benjamin Franklin

One great way to keep track of your opportunities and of what you want to teach other people is to keep a journal where you write down, draw, or even doodle impressions, ideas, and observations you come across.

I take notes in my journal every day. I have used this approach for years. I also draft letters to friends, jot down notes during conversations, scribble details on books I want to read, and describe plans I have for future projects.

Commit to keeping a log at least for the duration of the time you work through this book. If you write in a journal for just ten days, you'll create limitless opportunities to learn from yourself. Use the journal to become accustomed to writing as a method of seeing things in new ways. Record your questions, observations, insights, jokes, and dreams. You never know when inspiration will strike, but as you keep a journal, you'll find that it strikes more frequently.

If you don't have a journal or some sort of notebook, start by using the blank pages in the back of this book. If you buy a journal, spend time finding one that's the right size, shape, color, texture, and design for you. Will you carry it in a pocket, backpack, or purse? Are you enticed by plain pages or lined pages? Do you need the journal to have a pencil compartment? There are many styles to chose from.

Keep a log of your impressions for the rest of the day. You don't have to write constantly, but spend ten minutes in each of the next four hours to recall and describe what holds your attention, what you think about, and what you learn. Don't get discouraged if what you write seems superficial or goofy at first. Keep writing until something insightful occurs to you. If you're reading this before you go to bed, keep a log for the remainder of the time that you read and a few hours tomorrow morning.

Throughout this book, you'll also use this journal for various types of exercise and self-reflection.

Supplement your journal with scrapbooks or files on different topics of interest. Cut out and collect newspaper and magazine articles, or print information from the Internet on any subject that inspires you, including family, food, health, music, technology, or politics.

I write notes to myself on the left-hand pages and write for upcoming articles, books, or talks on the right-hand pages. This allows me to be both orderly and free flowing in one place and to see connections I wouldn't notice otherwise between the different types of work I do. Experiment with different approaches and you're sure to find your own style.

Overcome Learning Anxiety

> Learn what you fear . . . then make love to it . . . dance with
> it . . . put it on your dresser . . . and kiss it good . . . night . . .
> Say it . . . over and over . . . until in the darkest hour . . .
> from the deepest sleep . . . you can be awakened . . . to say
> Yes.
>
> —*Nikki Giovanni*

> When we draw back from action, we are often motivated
> not by humility but by fear of risk.
>
> —*Palmer Parker*

Some of you are thinking, "If it were really so easy to find my motivation, I wouldn't need to read this book!" If you're bogged down searching for your motivation, you might be sabotaged by anxiety or fear. Anxiety is an emotion that asks, "Can I *actually* learn this?" and, "What will people think of me once I know?" These can be scary questions, particularly if you've ever been made fun of because of your curiosity and exploration.

Many of us only know that we're feeling anxious when we find ourselves actively avoiding something or behaving in an uncharacteristic way.

For instance, writing something down that you have to give to someone else may cause you to sweat. Speaking in front of a group of people you don't know may push your panic button. Be aware of the reactions you have, and understand that they are an outward reflection of internal feelings. These topics, tasks, or activities stir past memories of failures or frustrations.

Each of us develops anxiety as a way to protect ourselves from something—past problems we don't want to relive, uncomfortable situations that we never shook off, or even imagined monsters that were going to devour us, yet never did. Anxiety is a deeply conditioned, automatic reaction to any feelings of being physically or emotionally unsafe.

As you become aware of your anxiety, you can learn to accept it, experience it, and free yourself from its hold.

When even an inkling of anxiety arises, say to yourself, "Okay, I'm anxious about this, let me figure out what's going on."

If you can face the anxiety instead of pushing it away or ignoring it and become familiar with what happens to you when you feel it sneaking up, perhaps you can sidestep it and move toward what you want to learn now.

Practice observing yourself each time you feel anxiety arise. Stop for a moment to ask yourself, "What am I anxious about?" Don't suppress the anxiety but, rather, allow it to present itself unrestricted so that you can look at it and figure out what to do.

Next, take the hint that your body is giving you to stop and break the response. Do something to relax. Go for a walk, sit down, close your eyes, or take a few deep breaths. Listen to music or think about something funny. I tell myself a certain favorite joke which makes me laugh every time. Find a joke like that for yourself. Pay attention to what might be activating this anxiety and see if there is another way to approach the activity that doesn't cause this response.

What Will You Learn?

To learn more about motivation, I've asked thousands of people, "If anything were possible, what would you learn?" The most common answers I hear relate to a sport or physical fitness, a second language, home and garden, or playing a musical instrument.

People also have many practical work- and life-based interests, such as learning how to use the Internet, speaking in public, finding a mate, training a pet, or improving their relationships with family and friends.

When I encourage people to learn about what catches their attention, I encounter all sorts of anxieties and excuses for why they don't follow through.

If you think, "I don't like working at the same speed other people do," find a rhythm that works for you. I offer specific suggestions on pace in chapter 9. If you think, "I'll never be good enough," realize that none of us are sure that we'll be as good as we hope to be, but if you never dare to take even one step forward, you'll have no chance to succeed. As you'll see in chapter 4, the small steps you take to learn something new will open you up to a much wider world and more opportunities to learn.

If you think, "I'm too busy with my spouse and children," consider getting them involved. Chapter 7 focuses on learning with other people. If you think, "I'm much too busy at work; I'll start when things settle down," recognize that in today's society, things may never settle down, and as you grow older, you'll be glad you spent time following your dreams.

And if you think, "I'm too old now; I should have started when I was younger," remember that it's never too late. As you'll see in later chapters, your learning power can *improve* with age.

When I talk with people who took up the challenge to learn—such as Pearl, who learned to hunt when she was sixty-one so that she could spend more time with her son, or Mike, who became a photographer to spend time outdoors, away from his desk—they report how it changed their perceptions of themselves. They gained confidence in their ability to learn even more.

Answer these questions:

What barriers prevent me from learning what I want to?

Full time job / position

What are the barriers inside of me?

Fear of failure / Anxiety

What are the barriers between me and someone else?

None

What are the big barriers around me?

Job, time, family sacrifices

Then, whatever your answers, take steps to address the barriers now.

2

Learn Your Nature

Learning is as natural to human beings as breathing, eating, sleeping, playing or procreating. And as far as anyone can tell, we maintain that natural capacity as long as any of the others.

—*Ron and Susan Zemke*

First consider, what is the matter; and then learn your nature, if you can bear it.

—*Epictetus*

Learning is a natural process, like breathing in and out. You learn easily every moment of every day—at work, at home, and while doing things that don't feel or look at all like learning.

If I asked you to describe a recent effort to learn something, quite possibly you would describe at least part of the experience as hard work or frustrating. Why the discrepancy? Perhaps you regard intentional learning as work, while exploring a new interest is fun.

For each of us, learning can be challenging, especially when the material, the situation, or the person teaching doesn't make sense. The question isn't *whether you can learn*. The question is *how do you learn*, and how do you restore the natural joy of learning to your everyday life in ways that match and support your natural learning style?

The learning styles assessment in this chapter provides you with an opportunity to learn how you'll likely respond under different circumstances and how to attain information in a way that best addresses your own particular needs. It also introduces you to the notion that your learning style spills over into how you communicate with other people as you learn.

If you're already familiar with your learning style and have worked through an assessment prior to reading *Learn More Now*, this chapter also offers specific tips on how to work with other people based on their learning style. Once you understand yourself, introduce the material in this chapter to the people you work with, live with, and spend time with each day. The more that people are familiar with their own natural way of learning, the more you can improve on how you live and learn together.

Road Map to This Chapter

Chapter 2 takes you to the following destinations:

▶ Learning about your learning style

▶ Mastering simple drawings

▶ Creating picture maps

▶ Improving your speaking skills

▶ Engaging your emotions

Lowdown on Learning Styles

> Before we can walk, talk, or write, we are filled with the ecstasy of learning.
>
> —*Bill Samples*

Anytime you begin something new—move to another town, start a new job, take up a hobby—there is something to learn. *Learning styles* refers to the ways you prefer to approach new information. Each of us learns and processes information in our own special way, although we share some learning patterns, preferences, and approaches.

By knowing your individual style, you can adjust your surroundings to make the most of the situation and to master new topics that might otherwise be difficult for you. Understanding your style may help you realize that other people might approach a situation differently than you do.

No matter what your style, at a young age, you were probably told by some well-meaning teacher to adjust that style: sit still, be quiet, stop daydreaming, quit doodling, or face forward. This meant that if you learned best by these means, you had no opportunity to engage yourself fully. If you're like most people, you still follow those rules.

Thankfully, even though you prefer to receive information through one sense more than others, you always take in some information through all of your senses. When one mode isn't available, you compensate with another—even though the sensation and the effect may not be as strong.

Learning style assessments classify how people see, hear, speak, and move through the world in order to learn. Whether we rely more on one sense than on another has a tremendous influence on how we interpret new experiences and affects our ability to succeed in what we work on each day.

What's Your Learning Style?

Take a few minutes to complete the following questionnaire to assess your preferred learning style. Begin by reading the words in the left-hand column. Of the three responses to the right, circle the one that best characterizes you, answering as honestly as possible with the description that applies to you right now. Count the number of circled items, and write your total at the bottom of each column. The questions you prefer will offer insight about how you learn.

1. Concentrating	Does seeing untidiness or movement distract you? Do you notice things in your visual field that other people don't?	Are you distracted by sounds or noises? Do you prefer to manage the amount and the type of noise around you?	Are you distracted by activity around you? Do you shut out conversations and go inside yourself?

(continued)

2. Visualizing	Do you see vivid, detailed pictures in your thoughts?	Do you think in sounds and voices?	Do the images you see in your thoughts involve movement?
3. Talking	Do you dislike listening for a long time? Do you often use words such as *see*, *picture*, and *imagine*?	Do you enjoy listening? (Or, maybe, you're impatient to talk?) Do you often use words such as *say*, *hear*, *tune*, and *think*?	Do you like to gesture and use expressive movements? Do you often use words such as *feel*, *touch*, and *hold*?
4. Contacting people	Do you prefer direct, face-to-face, personal meetings?	Do you prefer the telephone for intense conversations?	Do you prefer to talk while walking or participating in an activity?
5. Meeting someone again	Do you forget names but remember faces? Can you usually remember where you met someone?	Do you tend to remember people's names? Can you usually remember what you talked about?	Do you tend to remember what you did together? Can you almost feel your time together?
6. Relaxing	Do you prefer to watch TV, see a play, go to a movie?	Do you prefer to listen to the radio, play music, read, talk with a friend?	Do you prefer to play sports, knit, build something with your hands?
7. Reading	Do you like descriptive scenes? Do you pause to imagine the action?	Do you enjoy the dialogue most? Can you "hear" the characters talk?	Do you prefer action stories? (Or, maybe you don't even enjoy reading for pleasure?)

8. Spelling	Do you try to see the word in your mind? Do you imagine what it would look like on paper?	Do you use a phonetic approach to sound out the word? Do you hear it in your thoughts or say it aloud?	Do you write down the word to find out if it feels right? Maybe you run your finger over it or type it out?
9. Doing something new at work	Do you like to see demonstrations, diagrams, and flow charts? Do you seek out pictures or diagrams?	Do you find verbal and written instructions helpful? Do you like talking it over? Do you ask a neighbor?	Do you prefer to jump right in and try it? Do you keep trying? Do you try different ways?
10. Putting something together	Do you look at the picture and then, maybe, read the directions?	Do you like reading or talking with someone about it? Do you find yourself talking aloud as you work?	Do you usually ignore the directions and figure it out as you go along?
11. Interpreting mood	Do you primarily look at facial expressions?	Do you listen to the tone of voice?	Do you watch for body language?
12. Teaching people	Do you prefer to show them?	Do you prefer to tell them? Write it out?	Do you demonstrate how it's done? Ask them to try it?
Total	**Visual** _6_	**Auditory** _5_	**Tactile/ Kinesthetic** _1_

The column with the highest total represents your primary style. The column with the second-most choices is your secondary style.

My primary learning style: _____Visual_____

My secondary learning style: _____Auditory_____

Now that you know which learning style you rely on, read the following suggestions to see how you can boost your learning potential while reading this (or any) book.

If your primary learning style is visual, draw pictures in the margins, look at the graphics, and read the text that explains the graphics. Envision the topic in your thoughts.

If your primary learning style is auditory, listen to the words you read. Try to develop an internal conversation between you and the text. Don't be embarrassed to read aloud or talk through the information.

If your primary learning style is tactile/kinesthetic, use a pencil or a highlighter pen to mark passages that are meaningful to you. Take notes, transferring the information you learn to the margins of the book, into your journal, or onto a computer. Doodle whatever comes to mind as you read. Hold the book in your hands instead of placing it on a table. Walk around as you read. Feel the words and ideas. Get busy—both mentally and physically.

Are You a Visual Learner?

You can observe a lot by just watching.

—*Yogi Berra*

If you're a visual learner, you probably prefer to look at what you're learning. That's because you make sense of, remember, and process things you see. Pictures almost certainly help you understand ideas and information better than text or verbal explanations do. When someone explains something, you may create a mental picture. When you try to remember something, you may even see your own internal movie of what happened. Even when you use words to communicate with other people, you find those words by describing what you see in your mind's eye.

Although anyone with reasonable eyesight, no matter his or her learning style, takes in images faster than words and finds that pictures create an instant impression, visual learners regard this mode as more efficient than any other.

Rather than listening to what someone says, you may find yourself watching the speaker. Telephone conversations might be difficult because you're so accustomed to getting visual cues from people while they talk. To learn, don't just stare at a page. Move your body and your eyes to heighten your visual perception and your comprehension.

If you're a visual learner, you might wonder why you don't enjoy reading more; after all, books require you to look. Few visual learners I know are avid readers because most people process written information by hearing themselves say the words, not by creating a mental picture of what the words say. This process is more similar to an auditory learner's, rather than a visual learner's style.*

I learned that my husband, Karl, is a visual learner while we were dating. He has an encyclopedia-like knowledge of the animal world. My friends and I would try to stump him with questions about obscure animals, but he almost never missed a question or an opportunity to show off what he knew. This seemed odd to me because everyone I knew who specialized in seemingly little-known facts read all the time, and I'd never seen Karl read more than a weekend newspaper.

One day I asked him how he had learned so much about animals. He explained that Mutual of Omaha's *Wild Kingdom* was one of the few television shows his parents let him watch while he was growing up. Each Sunday his family gathered around the television to watch host Marlin Perkins wrangle with exotic animals from around the world. Although my family watched the show, too, I didn't remember all those facts and I didn't take a lifelong interest in wild animals. Karl has a vivid recollection of these shows because he is a visual learner who takes in information best from what he sees.

Mack, a photographer and a web site architect, jumps up during meetings to draw on a flip chart or a whiteboard. He is checking to see whether he has gotten the message or if the picture in his mind's eye represents what other people see. Frequently, it matches; sometimes he finds that it doesn't. After years of asking people to explain or describe something again, he is more apt, now, to ask for a picture or draw one himself. He has accepted that he needs pictures as much as other people need words. Now his specialty is to help companies use pictures to bring greater meaning to words.

---

*A small number of dedicated readers see words as pictures and are considered "visual text learners."

Woodleigh almost flunked out of school because she drew pictures instead of writing or reading her assignments. She never did find a way to succeed in academia, but she has managed to turn things around—and now makes her living by writing and illustrating beautiful children's books.

When Kavita, a visual communicator and the illustrator of this book, begins a new project, she cleans all the surfaces in her work area. She says that the visual clutter distracts her from getting started on new projects. Once she does begin, she posts her images on the walls to be able to see them from all angles and perspectives.

Tips for Visual Learners

These tips will help you learn from what you see. Write your favorite tips in ornate letters on a sticky note, and post it on your refrigerator door, the front of your journal, or your dresser mirror—anyplace that you see each day. Draw symbols and pictures all around the borders to help bring these words to life.

Add visual images. When you see a useful diagram, a sketch, a schematic, a photograph or a flow chart, cut it out and put it in a journal or in a folder marked GREAT IMAGES. Intersperse these into your reading materials to clarify a point.

Create charts. When you see a percentage written out, draw a pie chart or graph beside it to visually grasp its meaning.

Ask for pictures. When someone explains something to you, ask the person to supplement their words with a picture. Even a simple line drawing on a paper napkin can help you understand their point.

Doodle in the margins. Make book margins and your journal a canvas to sketch pictures of what you read. You don't need artistic skills. Simple sketches can help trigger the message as effectively as a detailed image. Draw what you see when you reflect on the subject.

Read what suits you. Seek out authors who use colorful and visually captivating language. Novelist Michael Crichton, for instance, did a terrific job with the visual details of *Jurassic Park*, so that many of his readers understood what the dinosaurs looked like even before they saw the movie.

Ask for a demonstration. Whenever you can, watch a presentation on how to create something. Be sure to look at the finished product, ask questions, and request that the presenters show you their favorite variations.

Use visual materials. Seek out instruction from videos, movies, and demonstrations, rather than from books or text-based web sites. Magazines illustrated with captivating photography will often prove useful, too.

Working with Visual Learners

If you work with visual learners, these tips can help you hold their attention and see what you're trying to convey.

Draw it out. Sketch a picture or a diagram when you need to elaborate. The picture doesn't have to be complicated or finely detailed, although it should show the connections between concepts.

Use colorful speech. Use language to paint pictures. Use colorful adjectives that focus on the senses. Tell stories to show what you mean.

Create visual interest. Gesture as you speak. Wear interesting jewelry or colorful clothing. Do what you can to help visual learners focus on you as you talk.

Add images. Boost people's retention by including drawings, graphs, and charts in any handouts or reports you create. When you deliver a presentation, don't waste words on your slides. Instead, use images to supplement what you say.

Look through their eyes. In our word-based society, visual learners may not feel appreciated or understood. Take time to draw with them, envision with them, and see things through a new and colorful perspective.

Are You an Auditory Learner?

We spend the first twelve months of our children's lives teaching them to walk and talk and the next twelve years telling them to sit down and shut up.

—*Phyllis Diller*

There are two types of auditory learners—auditory listeners and verbal processors.

The most common type of auditory learner, the auditory listener, learns by listening to other people and may even carry on mental conversations and resolve problems by thinking back on what people have said. The less-recognized type of auditory learner, the verbal processor, likes to say what he or she is thinking.

If you're an *auditory listener*, you listen intently to the world around you and glean meaning from sounds, intonations, and words. Constant noise or startling sounds, such as sirens and bells, may distract you. For the most part, you understand what people are saying to you, and you usually gravitate toward opportunities where you can listen to other people talk. You also may enjoy books because reading gives you a chance to hear the story in your *mind's ear.*

As an auditory listener, you're at an advantage in a word-based society, but even you can become overwhelmed when too much information comes at you.

If you're a *verbal processor*, you probably know intuitively that until you say something aloud or at least move your lips, you're not quite certain of your thoughts or their implications. In meetings or in classes, you may repeat what the facilitator has said and may feel a need to offer your comments, too. You're probably not trying to be disruptive and wish other people would realize that talking helps you to learn.

Verbal processors are at a distinct disadvantage in a society where polite people speak only when spoken to. This makes it even more imperative for verbal processors to understand their own learning style.

Carisa, a management consultant, can recite back an entire news segment she heard several days ago on National Public Radio. She is an auditory listener. Much of the information she retains is material she has heard, whether in conversation, on the radio, or on television—even if she's listening from another room.

Jim, a writer and a community leader, spends his morning reading the newspaper and then adds another dimension to what he's read by listening to the news on the radio. By using two different auditory techniques together, he remembers more and can use one method to help him focus on the other.

Angie, who runs a small family business, talks her way through nearly every meeting. She even talks to herself at the grocery store. A classic verbal processor, she keeps track of details and figures out what needs to happen next by giving voice to her thoughts. She sometimes has trouble with colleagues, who doubt her abilities, because they assume that she talks to herself because she's nervous. Actually, she talks more when she's comfortable, and talking helps her to understand situations in more meaningful ways.

Tips for Auditory Learners

The following tips will help you learn from what you hear and say. Write your favorite tips on a sticky note, and post it some place where you look each day, or share the idea with people you spend time with so that they can repeat it back to you.

Choose words. Don't rely only on reading—ask people to explain things to you. When you hear their words, you might notice subtle nuances that will help you glean additional meaning.

Listen to nonfiction books on tape. Even though books on tape may seem like a dream come true for auditory listeners, you might find that the pace of some fiction books is too slow to enjoy. Nonfiction, however, especially books that are difficult to understand in print, may prove to be helpful and more enjoyable to listen to because you can hear the author's inflections and tone.

Layer your listening. Because you assimilate information well through your ears and by hearing your own thoughts, you can benefit by putting the two techniques together. Try listening to someone talk about a subject, then read or talk more about it, and vice versa.

Use closed captioning. If you live in a family of television watchers but don't seem to enjoy it as much as everyone else does, turn on the closed caption setting so that you can read along with the programming.

Use notes to summarize. In a class or a meeting, taking thorough notes during a talk can interfere with your ability to hear what's important. Whenever you can, write during pauses or breaks and aim only at summarizing the key points, instead of trying to write out every detail.

Order conference tapes. Many conferences record keynote speeches for conference attendees and offer tapes to people who didn't attend the event. You can order these talks from the organization that sponsored the conference or from the service that does the taping.

Use words to trigger memories. When reviewing your notes, let the words trigger the memories of what you heard and play back the voices in your thoughts. Try to hear again the way the speaker said something. Where was the emphasis? What was skipped over?

Read from paper, instead of a screen, whenever possible. There is a fundamental difference in how your eyes and your brain process information on paper and onscreen, so your ability to comprehend, understand, and use the information is not equal. That's because most computer screens refresh at rates based on electromagnetic design, not on the visual operating system of your brain or the rate your eyes blink. As the screen pulses, you think you see a constant uninterrupted screen, but you don't.

Tips Especially for Verbal Processors

If you learn best by hearing your own voice, read the following techniques out loud to yourself.

Talk it through. Talk through the steps as you do something on your own. Read the instructions aloud as you go through the steps.

Pace yourself in meetings. Develop a pattern of first listening to other people before talking about what to do with the information. If you talk constantly, you won't have an opportunity to take in anything new.

Use the mute button. On conference calls, use the mute button on your telephone any time other than when you have a key point to make. This way, you can verbalize everything you're thinking without everyone on the call hearing you.

Repeat what you hear. Summarize what you've heard from other people to test whether you understood. Repeat telephone numbers as you hear them. Restate a person's name when you're introduced.

Find other people like yourself. In workshops or meetings, sit with other verbal processors (preferably off to the side, where you don't distract other participants) so that you can talk with one another throughout the program.

Tape yourself. Capture your thoughts and ideas with a tape recorder, but don't be so concerned with listening to the tape afterward—your own talking is what's important. The recorder, for that matter, doesn't even need to hold a tape. People around you will think you're talking for a very important reason—and you are: so that you can learn.

Talk to yourself. Talk through what you think, but first let other people around you know that you're talking to yourself whenever they hear you not using complete sentences.

Write it down. Write out your questions and comments during a time when you must be quiet, for instance, while someone else is talking. Later, meet with the speaker for a one-to-one conversation so that you can engage more fully with what they said.

Read aloud. Whether you're reviewing a simple memo, a book, or even a newspaper, read it aloud to yourself. Hearing your own voice is the key to taking in the information.

Working with Auditory Learners

If you work with auditory learners, use these tips to help them hear your message.

Talk together in real time. Find opportunities to talk in person to auditory learners rather than relying on e-mail or voicemail alone to communicate your ideas.

Especially for auditory listeners: Listen closely. Auditory listeners may not talk much, but when they do say something, it's probably important to them.

Especially for verbal processors: Let them talk. For this type of person, verbal processing isn't idle chatter. Find ways to support, rather than interrupt, their conversational style. Encourage talkative people to work together so that they can learn together.

Connect on the telephone. When you need to engage a verbal processor and can't talk in person, hold a conversation by telephone.

Share your concerns. If the commentary of the verbal processors is disruptive, gently let them know that their talking distracts you. Ask them to find other ways to express themselves during particularly inappropriate moments—maybe by writing down their comments. At the same time, work hard to create an environment where their style is honored and appreciated.

Are You a Tactile/ Kinesthetic Learner?

We were all eager in one way or another to fix the message in our bones and our muscles.

—*Raffaella Brignardello*

If you're a tactile/kinesthetic learner, you incorporate information through touch and movement. As a result, you may not thrive in traditional work environments because there aren't enough opportunities to hold things or move around.

You may make statements like, "Enough talking and looking. Let's get our hands dirty." In school, classroom discussions and written materials probably frustrated you, but you most likely caught up and even jumped ahead during lab time. Tactile/kinesthetic learners find it useful to role-play, participate in cooperative games and simulations, and work at hands-on projects.

How does this process work? The tactile system, prompted by receptors in the skin, gives us information about the size, the shape, the texture, and the temperature of what we touch. The kinesthetic system, activated through receptors in our tendons and the muscles, responds to movement. Your kinesthetic system recognizes, for example, when you're about to fall off a curb or when a dance sequence you're practicing hasn't been properly performed.

Years ago, I was trying to help a group of software engineers understand how information moved across the Internet. When I realized that these computer-savvy people weren't grasping this confusing concept through words or pictures, I borrowed several empty soft-drink cans that lined a nearby window ledge. We pretended that these were data packets as we moved them along the hallway to show how information flowed.

That helped some people get the concept, but it didn't help everyone. We eventually had the engineers themselves act as packets—each of them moving in different directions around the room. That made the concept clear to the rest of them. These simple actions allowed everyone to grasp the similarities between information moving along the Internet and people moving around the room.

Jay, a marketing executive, learns as he moves around. At conferences, he takes pictures because his camera keeps him at the center of the activity. "Walk with me," he says, as his colleague briefs him on the way to a meeting. It's not that he doesn't take in information through his eyes or ears—he just learns best when moving around.

Faye, an energetic realtor, loves her job most when she is walking around houses, running her hands over the walls, or touching the upholstery of a couch. Although she learns a little from her clients when they set up their appointment on the phone, she knows she will understand them better when they walk around a home together.

Ramona and Anya took a break from an all-day strategy session to walk around the block and get some fresh air. Once they started moving, they gained a new perspective on the subject of their meeting. Simply walking helped them to work through a problem they couldn't seem to resolve while seated at the conference table.

Austin's thoughts were elsewhere when he attended a class where he had to sit quietly and be still. His tone changed, however, when Tinker Toy–like Zome tools were placed on the floor for building models. While other people continued talking, he sat on the floor and began putting the pieces together—literally and figuratively. At that point, he was doing more than simply paying attention, he was finally seeing and understanding.

Judy has wanted to buy a travel outfit from a catalog for a long time but still hasn't been able to bring herself to do it. She makes her best decisions about clothing while walking among the outfits at the store, feeling the fabric, holding clothes up, and setting them beside each another. Without the ability to move around or touch the materials, she doesn't feel secure in her decision or learn enough to make a choice she knows she'll be happy with.

Tips for Tactile/Kinesthetic Learners

These tips will help you get a feel for how to move with things you want to learn. You too can write your favorite tips on a sticky note, then post it on the leg of your trousers. Glance down at it every time you walk. Swing a note to yourself on a mobile that hangs from the ceiling of your office, or tape it to a ball that you bounce up and down during the day.

Move around more. Practice walking around and reading at the same time to see if that helps you concentrate in a new, more powerful way. (Begin by getting up now and walking around while you read these tips.)

Find a new toy. Play with Silly Putty, a rubbing stone, or a stress ball to help reduce tension and keep yourself focused.

Take notes. Highlighting text and taking notes will get your arm moving and put your hands in contact with the meaning of what you read and write.

Use a mobile phone. Get a wireless telephone with a headset so that you can walk around as you talk. If you work in an office, there are new models of wireless headsets that will let you use your regular telephone but give you a wide area to roam.

Write, draw, and doodle. Doodle or make notes during presentations if you can't easily move around, walk, or pace. Merely putting pencil to paper will bring you new insight.

Write big. Create outlines and plans on a chalkboard, a white board, or chart paper. Bigger is better because you'll engage more of your body as you write.

Hold and flip. When you want to memorize something, write a key word or a question on the front side of an index card and a hint to the answer on the back side. Flip the card as you try to remember the message or work through the problem.

Working with Tactile/Kinesthetic Learners

If you spend time with tactile/kinesthetic learners, use these tips to move your message.

Try talking less. Tactile/kinesthetic learners can get bogged down by elaborate instructions and fancy pictures. Offer structure, but don't go overboard with your explanations.

Get moving. Take a walk together, toss a ball back and forth, build models, or simply move things around.

Give them a model. Tactile/kinesthetic learners like working with physical objects they can see from different angles.

Let them learn by trying. Tactile/kinesthetic learners are ready to work through things, even if they don't know what to do next or how it will turn out. They usually figure things out as they go along.

Be patient. Tactile/kinesthetic learners are, by definition, movement-oriented. Be patient with their tendencies to wander around, play with and try things, and frequently tap a finger, bounce a foot, or rock back and forth. They're doing this to help themselves learn.

When thinking about styles, try to think of them broadly, remembering that none of us learns in only one way. Also, when you have a choice about which mode to use, choose more than one. Consider writing and reading, doodling and writing down words, saying aloud what you write down, and looking at pictures while describing what you see. When you access information through several senses, you retain it in more than one part of your body and your brain.

Take Action with Learning Styles

Life is the art of drawing without an eraser.

—John Gardner

I encourage you to work through these activities as you discover how your learning styles influence your life. Each exercise is short and straightforward and will help you apply what you've learned in this book to what you do in the real world.

Adjust Your Approach

This first exercise can help you figure out how to apply what you've discovered about learning and motivation. Try the exercise yourself. Begin by making a list of topics you talk about with other people.

1. work

2. Sports

3. weather

4. Rules

Then insert the topics on the following lines as you consider different ways to approach the topics with various people.

How might I address the issue of _____ with
_____, who is goal-motivated and prefers an audi-
tory approach?

(Example: How might I address the issue of **writing an article** _with_ **Saman-
tha,** _who is goal-motivated and prefers an auditory approach? I might begin by
explaining what's in it for her and then talk her through the details, the deadlines, and the diagram requirements.)_

How might I address the issue of _____ with
_____, who is learning-motivated and prefers a
tactile/kinesthetic approach?

How might I address the issue of _____ with
_____, who is relationship-motivated and prefers an
auditory approach?

How might I address the issue of _____ with
_____, who is goal-motivated and prefers a visual
approach?

Learn to Draw

Because almost everyone benefits from seeing things, I find it helpful to
know how to draw simple shapes that convey meaning. If you're nervous
about your drawing ability, remember that no one expects you to be an
artist. You're learning the basics so that you can make your point with a few
simple lines.

Take some time now to practice drawing. In the following space, draw a
person, a place, and a thing similar to the pictures shown.

Now, draw a picture of something that will remind you of what you read in this chapter. It might be someone looking at a picture, watching television, or even drawing.

Improve Your Speaking Skills

Even if you're not an auditory learner, you can benefit from saying things out loud. That's because putting your thoughts into words forces you to focus on your situation. Speech is a tool that gives you greater awareness of your actions and makes it easier to adjust your approach.

It's curious how people tend to leave out what they already know or understand when they talk to themselves. We say only phrases and incomplete sentences to ourselves because what we say reflects our thoughts, which are, in themselves, incomplete. Most people tend to rely less on talking to themselves as their understanding improves.

So, go on—start talking to yourself! Next time you want to memorize a poem, recite it in a dramatic voice. Edit your writing by reading the text to yourself. Talk through a problem to find the solution. Or see if a story in the newspaper is much more interesting if read aloud.

Tell the book three differences between a traditional auditory learner and a verbal processor. (Yes, go ahead and talk to the book.)

1.

2.

3.

What Changes Over Time?

We are all the same age inside.

—*Gertrude Stein*

People in my workshops frequently ask whether learning styles change over time. Because they are based on physiology, they don't change all that dramatically after certain stages of growth occur. What changes are your senses. As these become more refined, you grow into your strongest preferences, and as your senses degrade, you adjust, compensating with the senses that are still sharp.

For example, most preschoolers tend to prefer tactile/kinesthetic approaches, partly because their gross-motor skills have developed the most. As children fine-tune and develop skills for writing, reading, speaking, and even visualizing, their natural learning preferences emerge. Auditory skills develop around the second grade, and visual skills mature around the third grade.

In contrast, as adults begin to lose their eyesight, they become less dependent on images to take in information. If their hearing decreases, they try to relate to their environment more through sight or movement. If you're not able to move easily or even reach out and touch something, you begin to compensate by using your other senses.

Face Your Emotions

Every second, a massive information exchange is occurring in your body. Imagine each of these messenger systems possessing a specific tone, humming a signature tune, rising and falling, waxing and waning, binding and unbinding, and if we could hear this body music with our ear, then the sum of these sounds would be the music that we call the emotions.

—*Candace Pert*

Learning requires more than being motivated and then activating your abilities to see, hear, move, or touch. To be an effective learner, you also must integrate your motivations and senses through your emotions. Sometimes this takes days. Other times, it happens very quickly.

Emotions help you determine how you feel. They're also associated with your movements, such as when you laugh, cry, tremble, shout, frown, gasp, lean, or run. Emotion comes from the Latin word *emovere*, which means "to agitate, excite, or move." Emotions also move inside your body, which is why your heart beats fast when you're scared.

Emotion is a sensing and a movement outward, one way that you communicate to the world around you important thoughts and needs. Your emotion is an external mirror of what you feel inside your body.

Try this experiment to feel what I mean. Stand up. Slouch your body in a depressed stance, drooping your shoulders toward the floor. Let your face and voice almost cry as you say in a miserable tone, "I can learn anything I want!" Doesn't it feel ridiculous, almost impossible to say without starting to smile?

Now stand tall. Put up your arms in a classic victory posture. Smile wide and say with enthusiasm, "I can't learn anything!" Once again, it feels ridiculous to say it in that pose.

Assume your victory stance again and cheer, "I'm ready to learn everything! Life is great!" Feel the invigoration when you combine encouraging thoughts with positive body position, movement, and energetic sounds.

Instead of slumping into the "I can't learn anything" posture, it's helpful to notice your emotions and use them to help you learn more. When you've had a bad day, for instance, take a bit of time to talk about what you feel, reflect on it, and remind yourself that you can start fresh tomorrow. If you try to ignore those emotions, you won't be able to concentrate or turn your attention toward what you want to focus on now.

If you're stressed, preoccupied, or afraid to make mistakes, even the best intentions won't bring you success. That's because emotions play a physiological role in the learning process. Remember when you blanked out on tests or forgot the name of someone whom you wanted to impress? This happens because when you're fearful or upset, a gland in your brain secretes a chemical that dulls the nerve receptors so that you can't pull information from long-term memory.

When you were young, if you were taught with methods that emphasized fear, you may think you need that emotion to be motivated to learn now. You should realize, however, that physiologically, it's the adrenaline from being afraid (that also comes from positive excitement) that helps you to learn. I'll address this more in chapter 5 on attention. Positive emotions cause your brain to secrete a different chemical, which makes you more open to learning easily and naturally.

3

Engage Your Body

My body was with me always. It walked with me, ran with me, slept with me, laughed with me, and followed me wherever I went. I spent a fair amount of time grooming my body, training it to perform and present itself in ways that were appropriate to my needs. . . . In class, my body would sit patiently while I was being educated.

—*Ken Dychtwald*

Many of us know, intuitively, that we listen to our inner voice more than we listen to anyone else. Gut feelings, educated guesses, ethical hunches, imagination, inspiration, grace, guidance from above, or intuition—whatever you want to call this prompting—are also as important in your understanding of what's going on as the logic you find in your inner voice.

If you doubt this, imagine not having your body as a guide. You wouldn't have that sensibility that you'd better not schedule that appointment for next Friday, that it's almost time to check on the pot roast, that Renee is more trustworthy than Ray, that a job you don't know much about is worth taking, or that today is the day you should call your mom. Many decisions like these may not have a logical basis, but they're vital to how you learn and live your life.

This chapter introduces you to natural and ageless approaches to learning that may at first seem unconventional and possibly even uncomfortable, but that can change the way you look at yourself. Diverging from the first two chapters in this book, which focused on *how you're unique*, this is the first of three chapters to introduce you to the workings of *how you learn* so that you can increase your potential to learn more.

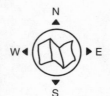

Road Map to This Chapter

Chapter 3 takes you to the following destinations:

▶ Learning in your whole body

▶ Accessing your inner knowing

▶ Getting out of your own way

▶ Getting off the chair

▶ Moving around

Help From Your Whole Body

> We tend to regard [thinking and learning] as a kind of disembodied process, as if the body's role in that process were to carry the brain from place to place so it can do the important work.
>
> —*Carla Hannaford*

> Our most refined thoughts and best actions, our greatest joys and deepest sorrows, use the body as a yardstick.
>
> —*Antonio Damasio*

If you're investing your time in learning more now, please don't waste another day believing the predominantly Western perspective that thinking and learning occur only between your ears. Contrary to science fiction movies and futuristic cartoons that show a time when heads in jars rule the world, you need your whole body to be intelligent.

Your brain and your body operate as a single entity; both play an integral role in your learning processes throughout your life. Scientists now have extensive evidence showing that you think, remember, and learn as much, if not more, in other parts of your body as you do in your head, and that the *mind* (the word used to describe what allows you to think) is located throughout the body, not only in your head.

Even though gross anatomy hasn't changed much for 200,000 years, modern imaging technology has begun to reveal the body's biomechanics, so our *understanding* is new and improved. For the first time in history, with new research in neurophysiology, neurobiology, somatics, quantum physics, and cognitive sciences, scientists now can show that all matter in the human body has a built-in intelligence, as well as the ability to think and learn.

To make sense of this, you first might need to recover from the fact that it probably contradicts everything you've ever been taught about learning. After all, most of us learned at a young age that learning is all in our heads. We think we're smart when we can find the right way to manage what we think and create rules to govern what we do. Although that can work in some situations, circumstances where one rule can supply the answer are becoming rarer each day, in every area of life. Sometimes, all you can do is admit that there simply isn't a rule that applies, and it's smarter to go with your gut.

Several years ago, I worked with a group of firefighters. They were quick to point out that they depended every day on this superior form of learning. They explained that firefighters don't weigh alternatives: They grab the first idea that seems good enough, then the next, and the next after that. To them, it doesn't feel like deciding or learning; it feels like doing their job.

Don't misconstrue what I'm saying. Your brain is the most complex organ in your body, serving as the processing center for many physical and mental functions. Before you can take that sip of morning juice, for example, the motor cortex in your brain completes an incalculable number of subconscious actions to coordinate your hand toward the cup. Before you can wake up your children, your vision center processes an equally incredible amount of information just to recognize their faces and identify your usual routines. Your brain, however, doesn't work alone.

To learn optimally, information flows instantaneously from your body to specific areas of your brain and back, at light speed, and from one area of your brain to another, each working separately and as one seamless unit. The thinking that you do with your body, similar to the thinking that you do with your brain, is part of a two-way system, up and down.

You could compare your whole body's learning capacity to a river that can flow in two directions at once. Sensory information enters somewhere along your body—through your nerve endings, your eyes, your ears, or your muscles—which then sends a chemical signal to another center, with each center farther upstream (or downstream) from the one before. Every inch of you is involved in sending, receiving, and then translating information. Cells that receive a signal or notice a change in the flow respond by making a physiological adjustment.

What your brain communicates to your body depends largely on what messages your body *sent first to your brain*. For instance, when you're happy, you smile, and when you smile, you feel happier. Faster than you can notice, every part of you has collaborated for the good of your whole being. Brain and body overlap and work together, often on the same thought. Your cells are literally talking to each other, and your brain is in on the conversation.

When I shared this with a group of middle-schoolers, one seventh-grader paraphrased it this way: "When they say 'It's like riding a bike,' the muscles in my legs remember how to pedal and my butt remembers how to sit, and my back knows how to balance, and my hands remember how to steer and all those thoughts go to my brain where it's assembled in 'ride the bike' terms." That's about right.

In the work I do, I call this *whole-body learning*. I chose that phrase because when you explain this to your family or your coworkers—and I hope that you do—they'll give you fewer weird looks than if you called it "body-mind" or "body-brain" learning, terms that researchers frequently use.

Integrate Intelligence and Intuition

[Intuition is] knowing without knowing how you know.

—*Lonnie Helgeson*

The mind can assert anything and pretend it has proved it.
My beliefs I test on my body, on my intuitional
consciousness, and when I get a response there, then I accept.

—*D. H. Lawrence*

The physical exercises throughout this book are designed to help you become more aware of how you learn, how you create new patterns, and how you establish new pathways to learn more. If you're considering skipping these, in an effort to learn even faster, let me assure you that these activities shouldn't take long, and they will help you establish your learning in more of your body than if you only read and took notes. I promise to keep the exercises short and focus on making the most of your time.

I suspect that you have always known you're more than what is in your head. To confirm this, try a simple activity.

1. Point to yourself.

2. Reflect on where you pointed.

3. Did you point to your head, to your body, or to somewhere across the room?

4. When you speak of "giving yourself" to someone else, what are you referring to? Do you give your brains, your heart, or your soul?

Try this with other people. Where do they point?

Work Together

This activity illustrates what happens when your brain attempts to override your body. The directions may seem odd at first, but should prove educational quickly enough.

1. Hold this book in one hand.

2. Lift one leg so that you're standing on one foot.

3. Notice the tiny adjustments your body begins making to keep you in balance.

4. Pay attention to when the teetering slows down, as your whole body gets comfortable and senses how to respond to itself.

Now put the book in your other hand and try balancing on the other leg. It doesn't matter if you hold the book on the same side or the opposite side as the foot you have raised. This time, serve as a commentator for your actions.

1. Hold this book in one hand and again raise a leg, so that you stand on one foot.

2. Point out when you're off balance by saying aloud or to yourself, "You're off balance!"

3. Express how long it takes to get in balance by saying something like, "Faster, faster, balance faster."

4. Ask yourself how you're progressing. "Have I improved 80 percent yet?"

5. Judge what you're doing wrong. "Why did I do that?"

As you sit down, reflect on which approach was more effective. Was it when you let your body adjust on its own or when you tried to make demands of your movements? Which was more enjoyable? Which way motivated you to want to do more and learn to improve?

When you tried to balance, you were reacting to things that don't enter your awareness. As you read these words now, you're still doing that. Your body forms to the chair where you sit, and you adjust your posture in response to thoughts your brain hasn't even noticed. Your hands respond to the size and the weight of the book in relation to how your arms feel as you hold it.

How Whole-Body Learning Works

The most illuminating learning tends to come from within your gut, your heart, and your back—literally. In the last decade, scientists have discovered messenger molecules—known as *peptides*, which were known to send and register information around the brain—in organs throughout your body, including your intestines, stomach, heart, liver, kidneys, and spine, and that these organs also send and register information.

Different peptides take on different roles in your physiology. The ones I refer to are neuropeptides, also called *neurotransmitters*, which create body-wide communication across your cells. There are almost as many of these peptides in your body as are in your brain.

These cells send signals (think of them as cell-based questions, seeking answers from other cells) that constantly run through your body. With every experience you face and every thought you have, your cells change both your body's and your brain's anatomy. No wonder each of us is completely unique. Your body-wide network of peptides that sends and receives signals is linked in unimaginably complex ways.

The network is also linked and communicates on a grand scale. To begin to fathom how grand, consider that there are 3,600 seconds in an hour and 57,600 seconds in a 16-hour waking day. If you have sixty thoughts per minute (which is far below your capacity), you have about 60,000 thoughts a day. Your 75 trillion cells, bound together by enzymes, proteins, peptides, and amino acids, communicate constantly and change what you learn about the world every second of your life.

Science suggests that intuition or whole-body learning is a real form of intelligence, and it works on a far larger scale than most of us have ever realized. It may be difficult to describe and is not always easy to get in touch with, but it can process information on a more sophisticated level than we ever dreamed.

It's Easier Than You Think

> It is always with excitement that I wake up in the morning, wondering what my intuition will toss up to me, like gifts from the sea. I work with it, I rely on it—it's my partner.
> —*Jonas Salk*

Learning with your body may come more easily than you expect and with practice, you'll begin to trust yourself in a new way.

Although consulting your inner knowing, something you can't always describe, may feel uncomfortable, your whole-body voice usually proves to be more right than wrong because it works without rationalizations. Can you imagine your gut saying, "Let me look at the budget before deciding if I should visit the doctor to reset my broken arm"? Probably not. That's because your body-based thinking cells know what's important and what needs attention now.

Researchers estimate that signals from these cells, which register as intuition, outweigh your conscious thinking on an order exceeding 10 million to one. In other words, your whole body is much smarter than your brain alone. And wise people regularly consult the smarter parts. Chess masters somehow know the right move to make, even if they can't articulate how they know. Great chefs have a sense of what spice goes with which dish, even if they haven't used a certain combination of ingredients before.

On a more basic level, have you ever felt stomach butterflies before an important meeting? Diarrhea when you felt afraid? That happens because the thinking cells in your stomach, right beside your digestive tract, are helping you learn to survive. The entire lining of your intestines, from your throat through your large intestine, contains cells with peptides and receptors. Emptying the digestive system prepares your body for fight or flight, both of which your body knows are easier on an empty stomach.

Body-based thinking cells also lead to a pounding heart, perspiring hands, neck pain, twitching eyes, chills, acne flare-ups, dry mouth, having the hair stand up on the back of your neck, and goose bumps, to name a few. These senses do more than remind you that you're uncomfortable; they care for you, educate you, protect you, and help you be strong.

You're probably not surprised that your body works this way. After all, when you hear a sound, your neck positions your ears to hear better. When a bug flies toward your eyes, you blink quickly. When you fall off a curb near moving traffic, your body jumps you back onto the curb before you even realize you've fallen off. Tasty food scents can cause you to salivate. When you see people you love, you may feel drawn to hug or kiss them. Your doctor even tests this system when she taps your patellar tendon, below the kneecap, triggering a response in about 50 milliseconds without consulting your brain.

Listening to this system, however, can be difficult unless you make a regular practice of it. Ask yourself:

What have I gone ahead and done, despite my whole body telling me to do something else?

What were the results?

How might I approach the situation today?

Harlan, a former U.S. statesman, explained to me the whole-body learning approach he uses when he starts to write something new. "I don't usually know just what I am going to say or how. I may have a tentative theme in mind—a happening worth relating, a fragment of fresh knowledge, a reaction to what has just happened in my community, in world affairs, or in my personal relations. I brood for several hours, dipping into my own notes and other people's writings. Then suddenly, quite literally in a flash, I know what I want to say and how to get it written. I've turned on (don't ask me how) my intuition—and it has imposed on my plodding, conscious, reasoned thinking a way of ordering reality that is clearly much more than the sum of its rational parts."

Clark, a cognitive psychologist, looked at me in astonishment when I began to explain whole-body learning. At first, I thought the surprise was because this flew in the face of the studies on which he had based a career. When I asked why he appeared so shocked, however, he replied in his usual even tone, "Marcia, while I've never studied such things, this should only surprise women. Men learn early that other parts of the body think." He had decided, however, many years ago, that he should separate these thoughts from his work.

Elizabeth, a gifted business manager, is dyslexic and sometimes has a hard time reading the details of labels that could alert her to whether something would be a good purchase or the terms of a deal would suit her. With some practice, she began to rely on how she felt and she learned to make decisions that way, based on feelings and hunches. After having used this method for decades, she says she can't imagine working any other way now. Even if she could read the material, she'd continue to make decisions from the assessment she does of the situation using her body, not necessarily her brain.

Lynn, a mortgage broker, prided herself on always following a logical path. When her husband was hospitalized because he had developed a large blood clot in his leg, she knew that she was worried about him but didn't imagine he was in serious danger. When she returned to work, however, the knot in her stomach wouldn't go away. She realized that her body had a different read on the situation than her rational mind. She returned to the hospital immediately to learn that her husband's health had rapidly deteriorated. He recovered fully over the next few weeks, but every day since then she's paid more attention to her whole body. She joked to me afterward, "If the rest of my body can help relieve some of my brain's work, and my body is here to pick up the other details, I'm being a fool not to put it to use."

Access Inner Knowing

> I don't read the paper & I don't watch TV & people ask me
> how I stay up with what's going on & I tell them breathing
> seems to help & since I haven't done serious damage to
> anyone yet, they usually leave me alone.
>
> —*Brian Andreas*

I hope that by now you're getting accustomed to the notion of engaging your brain, your body, and your physical senses to take in the world of information, in order to learn more.

Perhaps, however, you feel as if you already have too much information, not too little, in your life. Several years ago I found myself in this situation so I did something radical. I promised myself to stop reading newsletters, magazines, and professional journals for three months. I put some journals on a shelf for future reference (for when someone said, "You should take a look at . . ."), and others went into the trash or a box I looked through at the end of my hiatus.

With just this one change I gained a little time at the end of the day to relax and to open myself up to thinking, rather than constantly reliving what I had read.

Since I tried this little experiment, I've never returned to the daily, the weekly, the monthly, or even the quarterly publication dance. I haven't gotten rid of all of my magazines or newsletters, but I've stopped subscriptions to those I don't have time to read, that can be read online, that are available at my local library, or that I don't refer to regularly. I felt guilty about all the magazines stacking up that I never had time to read, and the guilt added to my sense that I wasn't learning enough right now.

Whenever you depend on outside sources for all of your learning, you may not cultivate the knowledge and the understanding you have within yourself. If you choose to keep a go-go-go routine, you might find yourself too exhausted to tap into what you already have. Get enough sleep, eat right, and take time for some balance in your life. This will contribute to your ability to hone that inner knowing.

If you let go of the expectation you have placed on yourself to keep up, you can get a feel for how crucial inner knowing is in your life. Information is important, but what you do with it is even more important. Take time to tap into your intuitive knowing each day. This approach is quite a contrast to searching the Internet for every imaginable solution. Sometimes you need to strike a balance between acquiring the information that's available through modern technology and accepting the wisdom that's available through your inner technology, by way of your intuition.

Likewise, most days don't include time for people to stop and reflect. As a result, you may feel as if you need to process information every second of the day.

In chapter 8, I offer a more comprehensive section on ways to reflect, ruminate, and let your inner knowing emerge.

Get Out of Your Way

> Don't believe what your eyes are telling you. All they show is limitation. Look with your understanding, find out what you already know, and you'll see the way to fly.
>
> —*Richard Bach*, Jonathan Livingston Seagull

To sharpen your whole-body learning, sometimes you just need to get out of your own way. To foster it in those around you, get out of their way, too. Here are ten guidelines:

1. ***Practice.*** Gut instinct is a form of pattern recognition. The more you practice, the more patterns you intuitively recognize. On a regular basis, list decisions you have made that turned out right—and mistakes, too. Then reconstruct your thinking. Where did intuition come in? Was it right or wrong? Are there patterns you can learn from the next time something happens?

2. ***Build a strong base.*** The wider and deeper you build your base of knowledge, the more useful your intuition. When you begin to grasp the language, the models, and the themes of a subject, you discover that you can finally get a sense of feelings that don't at first seem to fit anywhere.

3. ***Be there yourself.*** To gain your own sense of internal knowing, you can't rely on the impressions of your husband, your daughter, a

friend, an assistant, a planning committee, or a book author. You will need to participate and develop your own sense.

4. *Be willing to pay attention.* People come up with all sorts of reasons to ignore what their gut tries to tell them. Choose at least one activity each day to carry out *mindfully*—in the present, observing yourself, your feeling, and your surroundings without judging them—and pay attention to what your body tells you at each step. Over time, this can help you identify which sense reveals something you can't articulate, and you can listen to what that feeling has to say.

5. *Don't scare yourself.* I meet people all the time who think they're worse off than they were before they started to pay attention to their inner knowing. They're scared because, all of a sudden, they hear their inner voice question their decisions. They've simply noticed what has been going on inside all along. Those voices aren't competing; they're complementary. Awareness is the first step to making new choices. It's worth the temporary discomfort to get to know yourself.

6. *Tell stories.* Fictionalize a problem or talk about it as if it's happening to someone else. That can help you spot emotions and perspectives that you might not notice when you're in the middle of an event. Spend time at the outset of a project imagining that your efforts have failed and then gather the people involved to talk through the story of what went wrong. Next, play out the situation as if you were a glowing success. Children and adults alike can learn from this sort of storytelling and envisioning.

7. *Support whole-body learning around you.* Encourage people who hesitantly say, "I'm not sure . . ." with, "Tell us more." Remember that some people aren't verbal processors, and it takes a few minutes for them to gather their thoughts and talk about what they are feeling.

8. *Capture your hunches each day.* Bring more attention to your everyday flashes of intuition by writing them down in your journal, and then checking their accuracy. When you walk around, drive your car, or just lie in bed, remember to monitor what you're experiencing inside and note any inklings that arise.

9. *Be still.* Every day, devote a little time to stop whatever you're doing and, as best you can, eliminate all intrusions. Then close your eyes,

breathe deeply, and let your thoughts float like a log carried by the river. When you're still, you can eliminate restlessness and undirected energy. You can also become more aware of what's going on internally and externally.

10. ***Break from tension.*** Whenever you feel tightness in your neck, shoulders, or hands, it might be a build-up of tension from telephones ringing, e-mail beeping, computers crashing, people's demands, traffic, appointments, and too many to-dos. Try to focus on a tense area in your body. Breathe deeply. Say "Ahhh!" Squeeze that area and hold. Then release the squeeze, letting go of the tension.

Get Off That Chair

> You must learn to be still in the midst of activity and to be vibrantly alive in repose.
>
> —*Indira Gandhi*

> Nothing happens until something moves.
>
> —*Albert Einstein*

If you're sitting as you read this book, spend a few moments noticing how you're sitting now, and find a way to sit differently. You might sit in a different posture; move your chair to the right or the left, or stand up, move around the room, and pace as you read.

Even though you can learn while you're sedentary, staying chairbound for long isn't a good idea. For most of the last fifty thousand years, the human body has walked, run, skipped, and squatted. Although our bodies have recently adapted somewhat to sitting in chairs, we're physically more suited for other positions.

Sitting for a long time takes its toll on your body. It can result in poor breathing, back trouble, poor eyesight, body fatigue, and a limited perspective. These problems can reduce concentration and attention, ultimately resulting in learning problems.

A simple remedy is to move. Walk, swing your legs or arms, lean, kneel, squat, spin, or skip throughout the day. If work requires you to sit in one place, use breaks to stretch and move around.

Sitting in ergonomically designed chairs can also make a big difference.

The relationship between your legs and your spine determines healthy sitting. When that angle is between 120 degrees and 135 degrees, you balance your front and your back pelvis muscles so that you're less likely to feel fatigue. If you can't invest in a new chair, try completing an activity you usually sit through while standing, walking, or lying down.

Move Around

> Too many people confine their exercise to jumping to conclusions, running up bills, stretching the truth, bending over backward, lying down on the job, sidestepping responsibility, and pushing their luck.
>
> —*Anonymous*

Because of the relationship between your intelligence and your intuition, your body and your brain, exercise them all by frequently moving around. Something as simple as changing your posture can energize you and encourage your learning process. Although some people have reminded me that they're moving when their eyeballs move from side to side as they read or their hand glides across a sheet of paper, I encourage you to move around in a bigger way.

Stretch, juggle, jog in place, and walk to get water or just spin in your chair. Even sitting up straight or leaning way back will help you view the world from a slightly different perspective. Enjoy yourself and notice the shifts in the sights, the sounds, and the smells all around you.

Many people recognize that they experience their most creative flashes while walking, jogging, running, swimming, or just pacing. Basic motions activate cells that can trigger and change deeply ingrained communication pathways, helping you sense solutions, generate ideas, and learn new things.

Disciplined activities like yoga, tai chi, and even basketball can help you solve problems, increase concentration, establish balance, and enhance your ability to cope with physical and mental stress. Practicing any of these builds more connections, links, and pathways, which make it possible for you to do even more. If you're running around all day, consider all of the synthesizing you're doing without even realizing it!

If, however, you're saying to yourself, "I understand, but I can do that sitting down," please recognize that when you separate your activities into *sit-down-and-think activities* and *get-up-and-go activities*, you may prevent your body from generating insight, creativity, responsiveness, and skills that an active, moving, physical person offers the world. If you spend most of your day moving no more than to scratch your back, reach for a pen, or make a copy, you might be learning a little, but you're engaging only your brain cells and neglecting to integrate the whole-body signals that allow you to do more.

Position Yourself

Albert Einstein said that he made some of his greatest discoveries while lying on the floor. Have you recently tried learning from a prone position? If you have a clean floor, why not try it right now?

Over the years, I've experimented with dozens of specific movements to discover which activities might help me to concentrate, focus, and learn better. I also collect variations of these activities from participants in my workshops and from people who have visited my web site.

These moments all have one thing in common: They're simple and straightforward, and ask you to move in different ways than you normally would while you learn. You may already know about some of these movements from a creative physical education teacher or from attending a good yoga class.

Quick Moves

To add some quick exercise to your day, keep your abdominal and your back muscles taut whether you're walking around, sitting in traffic, playing with your children, or working out.

Twist from side to side as you brush your teeth or talk on the telephone.

Consider replacing your desk chair with a balancing ball. To sit straight and maintain your stability, you'll engage your midsection and the muscles along your spine.

Sitting Aerobics

Before we look at bigger moves, let loose for the next thirty seconds with some simple seated exercises. You can also do these wherever you are— at home, at work, in the car, in school, or even in a doctor's waiting room.

If you think they're sort of silly or fear that someone might be watching, think back to when you were three years old and everything was fun; you were willing to try anything. That's the mood for this exercise.

Start by looking around with your eyes, anywhere, somewhere new, at your feet, to the ceiling, or maybe under your desk. Then, move your mouth into a weird position—the weirder, the better. If you feel uncomfortable, close your eyes so that it feels like nobody can see you. Now twist from one side to another. Then, relax.

Walk Away

A brisk walk is more than exercise. It can increase your ability to produce *endorphins*—peptides that can reduce your pain and improve your mood. For most people, walking is easy to do, hard to get wrong, and requires no special equipment except maybe a pair of shoes. Walking is something you can do even when you're pregnant or injured, and most people can walk throughout life, even if they do it slowly or with assistance.

If you feel anxious or fearful, a quick walk can help take your thoughts away from your troubles and make you feel stronger and more able to deal with your situation.

Use these ideas to add more walking activities to your daily life:

▶ Park on the opposite side of the mall from your destination.

▶ Walk every aisle in the grocery store, even if you don't need anything in some aisles.

▶ At work, deliver things personally, instead of using interoffice mail.

▶ Go for a five-minute walk around the block when other people take their smoking break.

▶ Hide your television remote control so that you have to walk to change channels between shows.

▶ Play catch or hide-and-seek with your kids.

▶ Take the dog for more walks.

▶ Spend time with a toddler.

- Get up from your desk and take a three-minute walk around the halls every hour.

- Walk to your neighbor's house instead of driving.

- Get up and walk between meal courses.

- Go to the bathroom on a different floor than you're on.

- Cut your grass with a push mower.

- Use a wireless telephone and walk while you talk.

Find some activities that you can do no matter where you are, such as stretches you can do in a hotel room while you're traveling or isometrics you can perform in a car and at the post office.

Because exercise is most effective when you do it in a supportive atmosphere, these tips can enrich the effect:

Exercise with a partner for added encouragement and a little healthy competition.

Walk in an environment that appeals to you, such as by a lake, on a forest trail, in a park, or through your favorite neighborhood.

Vary your activities to enhance your whole-body development. For instance, walk some, jog some.

Breathe

Breathing deeply improves learning because the airways of your respiratory center are full of peptides that help make the connections between what you learn and your emotions.

Whenever I try to find my focus, I say to myself, "Breathe in through your nose and out through your toes." The breathing method that can help you focus and get unstuck works anywhere—standing in your kitchen, waiting in line, riding in an elevator, or even driving down the highway. This method can also help calm you down, control your nervousness, and allow you to focus on what's ahead.

This breathing method is quite simple:

First, tense each muscle in your body, going all the way up to your face and your scalp.

Second, relax each muscle so that your entire body relaxes.

Listen to your heartbeat and count how many beats for each in-breath, hold the breath, out-breath, hold the breath.

Then, just let yourself be. And listen.

Post-Check

After you have tried several whole-body exercises, do you notice a difference in how you feel? Ask yourself:

Am I more alert?

Do I have better focus?

Is my concentration better?

How about my comprehension?

Does my head feel clear?

Am I free of physical signs of stress?

Do I feel more relaxed?

To feel this way at any time you can get going. Take a break. Walk around the block. Nap. Daydream. Stretch.

Aging Bodies

> Now I've just gotten older, I've just gotten taller, and the little ones they call me a grownup.
>
> —*Carly Simon*

When I speak to groups, I'm frequently asked how whole-body learning changes over time. After all, the media is flooded with stories about mental decline, and most of us find ourselves struggling with memory as we grow older.

Many people assume that mental and physical abilities always decline over time; that after age twenty-five, we lose our learning capacity on a daily basis. Actually, our cells make increasingly complex new connections throughout our lives and throughout our bodies. Unless we experience catastrophic health problems, we're as capable of learning at age ninety-four as we are at four.

4

Open New Pathways

The purpose of education is to replace an empty mind with an open one.

—Malcolm Forbes

The principal mark of a genius is not perfection but originality, the opening of new frontiers.

—Arthur Koestler

When you learn, you build neural pathways and physical connections throughout your body that expand your potential to learn now and for the rest of your life. Learning, experiences, thoughts, actions, and emotions create more connections, building pathways, and then strengthen or destroy them. Billions of these exchanges take place continually throughout the body.

Your exact network of connections, at any particular moment, is determined by a combination of genetic makeup, environment, the sum of experiences you've had, and the sensations you're bombarded with now and every second into the future. What you do, moment to moment, influences how the web continually reweaves itself. These pathways change patterns every second of your life in response to everything you do.

This chapter introduces ways to create, strengthen, and extend your learning potential by releasing what no longer works and building new pathways throughout your body. These pathways will increase your receptivity and your ability to make sense of new experiences. Like the previous chapter, this one offers practical information on how to get the most from your inner workings so that you can enhance your potential to learn more. Yet it also provides you with an opportunity to examine your perspective and your pathways to determine which ones are worth keeping, losing, extending, or changing. The more you learn about your pathways, the more you can take advantage of the limitless opportunities around you every day. The more pathways to potential you have, the more successful you can be.

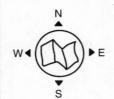

Road Map to This Chapter

Chapter 4 takes you to the following destinations:

▶ Widening your pathways

▶ Gaining another perspective

▶ Unlearning

▶ Creating more space

▶ Finding your direction

Pathways to Potential

> There is great irony in the fact that we have spent most of the last half millennium distancing ourselves from the pre-eminent learning system on this planet—nature itself— at the very moment when we most need to emulate it and reintegrate within it.
>
> —*Joel Getzendanner*

You have the power to continually rewire your pathways and learn, not only through studying, but also through experiencing, thinking, taking action, and moving. Every time you choose to solve a problem creatively or think about something in a new way, you reshape who you are and increase your potential to learn. The more pathways, the more connections; the more connections, the more access you have to understand and appreciate the world around you.

The more connections you make with people, concepts, experiences, and the environment, the more pathways you create. You create connections between your pathways by tackling activities that are unfamiliar to you. Maybe you have always wanted to learn to play a musical instrument, dance a new step, build something such as a bird house, or make the best chocolate chip cookies in the world. Maybe you have a burning desire to study philosophy or talk with provocative people. I personally want to learn to play the bass fiddle. In addition to creating pathways, new activities will make your life more interesting. It's never too late to start.

How Do Neural Pathways Work?

When a baby is born, it has millions of neural connections waiting for specific assignments. Even though the basic functions you need to survive (heartbeat, temperature control, and breathing) are already connected, you pave more pathways from what you learn—the environmental factor in your life. As the world makes demands, you enlist many connections for specific jobs, like babbling, seeing, remembering, or throwing a toy.

When you face new experiences, your pathways form new branches and connections. But what of pathways and cells you don't use? During several critical stages in your growing-up years, couch potato–like cells die off, while those cells that you exercise get stronger and develop more connections. Links that are weak, are unused, or simply don't fit anymore are pruned back, leaving you with only the most efficient connections. For optimum physical and mental development, this is why it's particularly important to expose children to as many new experiences as possible.

You increase your efficiency through learning, practice, and moving around. You make new connections each time you add information or experiences to your repertoire.

A process called *myelination* also increases how fast you process that information. A fatty substance called myelin coats neurons in your central nervous system every time they're used, making them more efficient.

With each message you send and receive across a specific connection, the stronger that pathway becomes. New thoughts blaze a new trail, making it easier for subsequent messages to fire along the same path. The more the path is refired, the more permanent the message and the new learning become.

Gain a New Perspective

We always seem to come to situations with
our history firmly entrenched, our minds
partially made up, and our own perspective
strongly in view.

—*Judee Humburg*

Soar, eat ether, see what has never been seen; depart, be
lost. But climb.

—*Edna St. Vincent Millay*

To increase your potential to learn, try to see the world in a fresh new way
each day. Changing perspectives helps you to see from various viewpoints
and from different angles or places.

Whenever you widen your perspective, you increase your ability to
learn. Look a little higher or lower and you'll see a different view.

Tell yourself, "Today I will think new thoughts, create new associations, and develop new and broader perspectives. I will approach the
world in a deeper, truer, richer way." If you commit to doing this, for even
a few minutes, you'll begin to expand your pathways at least a tiny bit.

These ten tactics can help you change your perspective now.

1. ***Change locations.*** Whenever you move, you get a different perspective. Learning in different places helps you develop recall flexibility. Your environment and the exact location where you first hear,
   see, or experience something influence what you recall and then
   learn. When I work with groups, I always have people move to a different side of the room after a few hours. This ensures that people
   see things from a novel and unbiased point of view.

2. ***Turn the world upside down.*** On a dry, sunny day, lie on your back
   in a parklike setting, viewing your surroundings from this new perspective. Passersby will seem upside down, and you'll see nearby flowers from another side. Taking time to view the world from a fresh
   perspective offers you rare moments of wonder. How differently must
   a squirrel learn about the world in comparison to a bird? Perhaps as
   differently as a person who drives a car compared to one who flies a
   blimp.

3. ***Work back from the future.*** I worked with new employees in the service department at a large department store chain. On their second day of work, with the aid of a full list of common issues, we had them answer support calls, many from irate customers. After only a few calls, the new employees quickly grasped that they had plenty to learn. From then on, they were very receptive to advice, coaching, and lessons from coworkers and instructors on how to handle difficult situations. I've used a similar activity with salespeople and line workers in a manufacturing environment. By seeing the end result of their work, they understood where to begin.

4. ***Broaden your reach.*** Suppose you wanted to explore career options. If you usually get advice from only one or two people, instead make a list of everyone who might provide help. Before tackling this list, begin by asking trusted friends for their perspectives and who they would suggest you add to your list. Besides getting a more detailed picture of what you can expect from each career choice, you'll see all the possible permutations. Every person's opinion will broaden your view.

5. ***Challenge your biases.*** My dad used to ask me, "What *can't* you do?" He did this to help me see that I could do almost anything. One day I finally found a reply: "I can't walk through the sun unassisted." That ended this conversation, at least for that day. His challenge allowed me to see, for the rest of my life, that I could do whatever I set out to do.

6. ***Get out of your comfort zone.*** Have you ever tried to fold your arms opposite from the way that you usually fold them (with your dominant hand on top)? Try it now. It probably feels a bit awkward. When you try something new, it's natural to feel uneasy about it and pull back. To e-x-p-a-n-d your comfort zone, start with some simple challenges to gain confidence for larger things.

7. ***Do familiar things in a different way.*** If you changed one routine activity in your life each day for a week, you might be surprised at how easy change would become. You would see that uncomfortable feelings are often a sign that you're learning something new. Changing old habits is a terrific way to stretch yourself. For instance, drive a different route home, shop at a different grocery store, order

something from the menu that you've never tried before, or sleep on the other side of the bed. Consider changing the part in your hair, shaving with your other hand, getting to know someone who is different from you, or putting on your clothes in another order. Make an effort to experiment with one thing each day.

8. *Walk a mile in someone else's shoes.* When you can see your work from another angle, such as from your children's perspective, from the perspective of your customers, or from a different layer of management, you learn a new way of understanding the value of what you do and how you do it. To try this for yourself or in a group, first let other people know that you'd like to swap roles with them. For instance, if you're interested in having children, offer to baby-sit a family friend's kids (at first, for a short time). At work, if you want to learn more about another job, offer to shadow someone who has that job or even work in another group for a few days. Often, the best perspective comes when someone needs your help and you volunteer to fill in with whatever they need.

9. *Find the hallway perspective.* Sometimes you can find a different perspective as close as the hallway outside of wherever you learn. In an office, consider posting a whiteboard or a chalkboard beside the water fountain, so that you can illustrate ideas and talk with whoever you meet there. In your home, keep a pad of paper near the dinner table, the kitchen sink, or wherever people congregate so that you can compare perspectives with your family. Home Depot holds frequent question-and-answer sessions between employees and managers, in which both groups ask each other questions. At Microsoft, we held "fire drills," where people met and talked about what they saw as upcoming issues or challenges, so that we could enlist the help, the perspectives, and the resources of other people.

10. *Talk about learning moments.* At work, ask your coworkers to start each meeting by completing the sentence: "Since I last saw you, I learned . . ." At first, you may hear some whining, but over time, people might begin to share what they've learned. At home, ask each member of your family to begin meals (or car rides, or whenever you get together) with the same sort of simple learning statement. You can modify this to be, "Since our last meal I learned . . ." "Since the

ride to school . . ." whatever makes it memorable and fun for every-one. The first time we did this at our house we heard hilarious answers. "I'd rather not have learned that we're out of toilet paper upstairs," and "I learned that the dog's stomach doesn't handle cheese all that well." The purpose is for people to think about what they see and experience as a chance for them to learn something and then share it with other people. This can become a lifelong habit.

Inventory Your Perspective

> In the perspective of every person lies a lens through which we may better understand ourselves.
>
> —*Ellen Langer*

The following questions can help you check your perspective about learning so that you can extend and connect your pathways in new ways. They are designed to help you think about yourself. These can be challenging questions, so take time to think about each one, or talk about them with other people, such as with your family at dinner tonight or with your coworkers at a meeting tomorrow. You also might want to write the answer here after each question, in your journal, or on the book's back pages.

How or where did I learn what I currently know about learning?

OJT

What topic did I know nothing about five years ago that I am expert in today? *Counsely*

How did I learn that much? (Did I attend a class, watch a video or a TV program, read an article, have a conversation about it, or base what I know on years of anecdotal evidence?)

School, Read, OJT

Have I put my understanding into practice, witnessed it working, or watched someone else do the same? *yes*

If I'm unsure how I learned what I know, do I still feel confident it's right and reliable? *Somewhat*

How strongly do I trust my knowledge?

Strongly

What are my passions? What topics have I wanted to learn?

fairness,
Business,
teaching,

Do I learn in a different way than I did as a child?

If so, how? *practical experience, read*

What makes learning boring to me?

Too much Reading

What makes learning interesting?

Hands-on, practical

What else have I done to learn about how I learn?

How do I determine my learning needs?

Do I focus on the current reality? Do I hold the big picture in a wide angle? Do I mix the various perspectives?

Sometimes

Clearing Space

To be fully free to create, we must first find the courage and willingness to let go. Let go of the strategies that have worked for us in the past. Let go of our biases, the foundation of our illusions. . . . You will find it is not a one-shot deal, this letting go. You must do it again and again and again. It's kind of like breathing. You can't just breathe once. Try it: Breathe just once. You'll pass out. If you stop letting go, your creative spirit will pass out.

—*Gordon MacKenzie*

> The illiterate of the 21st century will not be those who
> cannot read and write, but those who cannot learn, unlearn
> and relearn.
>
> —*Alvin Toffler*

Sometimes you need to change, rework, or prune the pathways you've already cultivated, release what you know, and seek out new paths. This is similar to the way you maintain a garden. If you want your plants to thrive, you periodically remove the weeds. In the case of learning, it's helpful to clip thoughts, beliefs, or behaviors that get in the way of your growth. When you can let go of some of what you know, do, and believe, you free up space to learn more. Without weeding, you can become stagnant. Take time to pick through things you've learned in life that are no longer useful.

I remember going to a small circus at a local community center when I was twelve. There I saw a real elephant up close. When it wasn't performing, it was tethered to a stake in the ground. I couldn't believe that this small stake held such a huge animal. My mom pointed out that it wasn't the stake holding the elephant there at all; it was the *idea* of the stake. Now I realize that it was the *pathways* of the stake. The elephant believed that it had to stay there because of its previous experiences and the perception that it was stuck right there.

Although it may sound counterintuitive, what you have seen influences what you think there is to see, so you think and learn less. What you know today may prevent you from paying attention because you think you already know what comes next. We tune out what we think we know because we already have so much to think about and focus on. The problem is that we can mistakenly ignore information that should replace what we've learned that's no longer true.

Unlearning

> It ain't what you don't know that gets you into trouble. It's
> what you know for sure that just ain't so.
>
> —*Mark Twain*

Unlearning can help you become open to new insights, new knowledge, and new learning. You can't physiologically unlearn anything, erasing the existing neural pathways, but you can create the equivalent of a mental attic and put a sign on the door that says, "Things I know that are no longer so." You can replace what you do or have learned with something else.

The process of learning how to unlearn doesn't need to involve much time or money. It isn't always necessary to hire an outside coach or spend hours in psychotherapy. You can recognize on your own how to unlearn what no longer works and decide to build pathways to what does.

The process of unlearning involves becoming more aware of the assumptions you make, the values you apply, the positive and the negative feelings you experience when situations confirm or challenge your assumptions and values—and the way you look at what's going on.

One summer in college, I worked for a local nonprofit alliance. Each day, a group of us was dropped off in a Wisconsin town, where we went door to door, telling people about the work of the organization and asking for their signatures on petitions. We focused primarily on lowering energy rates and cleaning up waterways. I took the job because at the time I was an active white-water canoeist and I knew something about the rivers in the state. Also, I wanted to learn how organizations like this worked, and it seemed like an interesting experience.

Each afternoon, I would knock on someone's door and recite my spiel. "Hi, my name is Marcia and I'd like to ask for only five minutes of your time to tell you a little about . . ." Twenty years later, those words roll out exactly as I had said them a thousand times. One day, about a month into the job, our manager, Chuck, came into our office before we went out and handed us each a slice of bologna. He asked us to put it in our left shoe. Wisconsin doesn't reach temperatures in July like St. Louis, where I grew up, does, but it was warm that day and this sounded unpleasant. All the same, he asked us to do it. I don't recall if, at the time, he explained why, but we followed his request.

At the first house, I knew why. Instead of saying the same phrase, in the same way, while flashing a bright smile, I needed to rethink every word. I had to have an authentic conversation with each person I met. That bologna made me forget what I had rehearsed and helped me do something much better than before. The next day, without the bologna, I found other sources of inspiration to rework how to do my job. The new ways were so much more interesting, engaging, and rewarding that I didn't go back to my tired old opening.

What can you do to start unlearning now? Write down something you would like to learn differently and think about novel ways to unlearn it.

Can you replace what you have known with something new? Might you adjust your underlying beliefs by looking from another perspective?

Here are ten approaches you can use to unlearn what no longer works.

1. *Let go of your past.* Your willingness to let go, take risks, face situations you never have before, and challenge your own belief systems allows you to find better methods. Branching out can prove difficult, though, because comfortable habits are familiar and easy—and you have probably grown attached to them. Yet, unless you release them for long enough to break them as habits, they will limit your potential. Does your new coworker remind you of a micromanaging boss from your last job? Let go of thinking, "You remind me of someone, so I'll interact with you the same way I did with that person." Try to replace that impression with a new one. If you're not careful, the old memories will limit your chances for new relationships. Give people a chance to be themselves, and learn from who they really are.

2. *Start from the beginning.* Sometimes activities that are similar to each other create the mistaken impression that they're the same activity, so we never give ourselves an opportunity to truly learn what's different. Take, for example, the case of a husband-and-wife team who attended my kayaking class. The man was a canoeist and found it almost unbearable to let go of what he knew about canoeing in order to learn to kayak. He spent a good portion of his early lessons trying to compare the two types of boats. Then he tried to use canoe strokes that he was certain would also work in a kayak. As a result, he repeatedly found himself facing the bottom of the swimming pool where our class took place. Only when he accepted that what he knew might not be as useful as what he needed to learn did he begin to create the pathways he needed to kayak. Meanwhile, his wife, a complete novice, made significant progress from the first day.

3. *Notice patterns.* All of us have a tendency to repeat things that worked for us in the past, even when they no longer work now. Repeating what works is a survival skill, a natural defense mechanism based on efficiency so that you can pay attention to what's new. This isn't always a bad strategy. When you have an urge to do something over and over, though, it can become obsessive and you stop learn-

ing anything new. You begin to think that you must have or must do something in a certain way. Try instead to notice the pattern so that you can adjust it. Raise your self-awareness by asking yourself, "What will happen if I keep behaving like this? Do I want to act this way for another ten years?" If not, it's time to learn new patterns.

4. *Stay open.* Unlearning doesn't require you to toss out all your accumulated experiences, but, rather, it asks that you stay open to different ways of getting things done, instead of presuming that one way is better than another. Take, for example, a parent moving into a new school district. She needs to learn about the new schools and the PTA, at the same time that she's unlearning the mind-set and the procedures of the system she and her children left. Her refusal to unlearn old rules will leave her unprepared. By thinking, "This is how we did it where we used to live," she might miss great learning opportunities for her family and never quite completely move in. If she goes in looking at how the new system works, she'll be ready for anything.

5. *Look for mirrors.* Make it easy for your family, friends, boss, coworkers, and employees to give you feedback by asking for it. The more people you have in your life who help you reflect, the greater your chance of gaining an accurate sense of how other people perceive you and which behaviors you ought to adjust. During Friday lunch meetings with his team members, John, a scientist, focused on what they did well, what they did wrong, and what they learned from it all. A primary objective was helping the team learn and unlearn. At one meeting, some team members casually remarked that whenever they saw John make a certain face in response to someone's idea, it was obvious that the idea didn't stand a chance. John had the next meeting videotaped. Sure enough, he saw for himself that he did sometimes wear a disapproving expression. From then on, whenever that feeling washed over him, he worked to change his facial expression and to listen more attentively to the other person's views.

6. *Make a replacement.* Another way to unlearn is to replace what you have known with something new. You constantly layer new information and experiences over old information. For instance, the name of your new doctor covers the name of the one you used to go to, your current home telephone number supersedes one from your last house, and this information becomes difficult to retrieve again

without a current connection to them. Ask yourself, what could I do with my time, money, and energy instead of what I've done so many times before? Could a replacement activity lead to a better quality of life for me and for those people I love?

7. *Be annoying.* To unlearn a pattern, deliberately repeat it over and over until you're completely aggravated by it. For verbal patterns, take ten minutes a day to stand in front of a mirror and repeat the offending phrase in an audible voice. If it's "uh," repeat "uh, uh, uh, uh, uh." You will likely grow tired of hearing the word and will find a substitute to use.

8. *Change your perspective.* Appreciate what you encounter for what it is, separate from your perception. Look at circumstances from someone else's perspective, in reverse order, as if you were new to the situation, as if you were bored, newly enthused, or even totally confused by what's going on. Your change in perspective will help you change your viewpoint because it will seem as if you're seeing it with new eyes.

9. *Notice the situation.* Figure out what conditions, times, places, and even people repeatedly lead you to a certain practice or pathway. Does talk of feelings trigger you to tune out? Does your doctor make you so nervous that your mouth dries and fills with stammers instead of clear questions? Does the mere sight of a computer cause you to consider quitting your job? Pay close attention to what situation, specifically, causes this reaction so that you can look to learn an alternate response.

10. *Create variations.* Combine and recombine your approaches to learning, while noticing the infinite possibilities in every situation. As you consider all the options, you can combine them into new choices that might be better than approaches you've used before.

If you think you'll never be able to remember these tips when it's time to unlearn, write yourself a visual reminder note. Make a list of those guidelines you want to try. Write the list in your journal or on a sticky note to post on the computer, the TV, the dashboard, or your desk—anywhere that will prompt you to spend more time thinking about the new activity you want to adopt, so that you can practice it right then and there.

Reflect on anything you've unlearned. Ask yourself:

What assumptions did I have at one time that I subsequently changed?

What once held me back that no longer holds me back today?

What did I once believe that is no longer true?

Which approach will I try, to replace outdated information?

Whom will I ask to point out patterns that no longer suit me?

Find Your Direction

> I find the great thing in this world is not so much where we stand, as in what direction we are moving.
>
> —*Oliver Wendell Holmes*

As learners, we differ in the order we prefer to receive and review information. Some people learn in a linear fashion, by taking a series of small incremental steps toward a goal. Other people learn in a more global fashion, first grasping the big picture and then linking together broad concepts in large leaps.

When you feel that you're receiving too few details or you can't grasp the larger concept, this might indicate that information is mismatched with your direction style—something that is usually easy to realign.

Everyone has both global and linear qualities when processing information, but some of us have a distinct preference for one over the other.

Most people assimilate and apply knowledge in a global way—up to 60 percent of the population consists of global learners. Only about 30 percent prefer a linear approach to learning. The rest integrate both global and linear styles, shifting from one approach to the other, depending on what they are trying to learn.

What's Your Direction Style?

Take a few minutes to complete the following questionnaire to assess your preferred direction style. Compare the two side-by-side responses and circle the statement that applies to you right now. Count the number of circled items and write your total at the bottom of each column.

I focus on the big picture.	(I focus on the details.)
I skip around when reading a book.	(I take things in sequential order.)
(I like a holistic approach.)	I like to make successive tries.
I like to take breaks.	(I like to be persistent.)
I generalize.	(I like to talk specifics.)
I prefer informal structures.	(I prefer formal design.)
(I tackle many projects simultaneously.)	I pursue one project at a time.
I like a multidisciplinary approach.	I like to focus on a single discipline.
(I like to look at the overall effect.)	I like to look at specific parts.
I like to synthesize.	(I like to analyze.)
I tend to look at themes.	(I tend to look at the particulars.)

Global Learner Total _4_   **Linear Learner Total** _7_

My direction style: _Linear_

If you're a global learner, you like to see the *big picture* before you begin looking at the details. To other people, it sometimes seems that you ignore the details, when actually you're looking for the bigger ideas—and you have no way of making sense of the details if you don't understand the overall concept first.

If you're a linear learner, you appreciate a *step-by-step* buildup of information in a certain sequence, and you like each step to follow logically from the previous one. You probably prefer facts and statistics to help you decide whether you want to learn more.

Are You a Global Learner?

Essentially, if you know who you are, where you are going, and what you want, then it is not hard to deal with inane bureaucratic details, trivialities, and constraints. You can simply disarm them and make them disappear by a simple shrug of your shoulders.

—Abraham Maslow

If you're a *global learner,* you approach information in big strides, incorporating material without thinking much about the connections, and then suddenly you sense how it all fits together. Sometimes, you may not be able to continue a conversation or reading when you don't see the point of it all. Once you do grasp the overall concept, though, you can quickly solve complicated problems or combine ideas together in original ways.

Are you wondering if everyone does that? You may conclude that you're a global learner if you've ever felt flustered and then, in a sudden flash, you understand. What happens *before* you grasp the meaning, however, determines your direction style.

If you're really a global learner, you probably need to understand how your actions relate to prior knowledge and previous experiences before you'll spend time with the details. This can become exasperating at times because when most people give directions and tell stories, they begin with the details and lead up to the big finish even though you needed that punch line up front.

Many years ago, I worked with a classroom of grade school children as they went through a history lesson. One student was looking out the window when the teacher called on him. She asked, "Who was the first president of the United States?" The daydreaming student replied, "I'm going to ride my skateboard in the park after school."

The teacher, disappointed with the student, asked why he thought that was an appropriate answer. Much to the teacher's surprise, he said, "You asked, 'Who was the first president of the United States?' That was George Washington, the guy on the dollar bill. I got my allowance yesterday so I fixed the wheel on my skateboard. After school I'm going out to skate." Linear-style teachers face global-style learners every day.

Tips for Global Learners

Here are a few tips to help you see the big picture.

Ask questions. Try to find out more about the overall concept. Ask questions like, "What's the big picture?" and "Can you give me a quick overview?"

Listen for the big message. Focus on concepts and long-range goals first, and get the details later. Separate what you need to know from what would be nice to know.

Read from big to small. Before you begin any book, study the introductory paragraph and skim through each chapter to get an overview. This may seem time-consuming, but it might actually save you from having to review individual sections later.

Manage your time. Immerse yourself in one topic for a large block of time, rather than spending a short amount of time on many different issues throughout the day.

Tips for Working with Global Learners

If you work with global learners, these tips can help you get your message across.

Begin at the end. If you're a linear learner, don't assume that your straightforward approach will work with global learners just because it makes sense to you. Offer your summary as a brief overview to help global learners orient themselves to the subject.

Ask for links. If you work with someone who seems to jump around from topic to topic or skips steps, you may have difficulty following and remembering. Ask for segues with questions such as, "How do those ideas relate?" or "How did you get there?"

Paint a picture of success. When setting out a project to complete, explain what success will look like. If you have no sense of outcome, discuss one or more of the general goals.

Appreciate variety. Global learners are likely to vary their strategy, change the size of the project or find alternative ways to work. Appreciate the outcome and its novelty, even if it's not the way you would have done things.

Offer models and resources. Provide global learners with existing models, and then give them an opportunity to design and develop their own models or results. Also, make available as many resources as possible, because they may never directly ask for help.

Are You a Linear Learner?

Going far beyond the call of duty, doing more than others expect—this is what excellence is all about. And it comes from striving, maintaining the highest standards, looking after the smallest details and going the extra mile.

—*Perry Paxton*

If you're a <u>linear learner</u>, you know that you don't need to understand something completely to continue learning. What you do want, however, are plenty of details and facts, and you probably don't rely on learning through stories or illustrations. You like step-by-step instructions and solving single-answer problems.

You obtain new information in small pieces and group similar topics together, which makes it easy to answer questions about a particular subject. You can solve problems even when you don't completely understand the material, but when someone asks you a question about another situation, you may feel jarred, at least momentarily, by the quick switch.

Likewise, linear learners sometimes have trouble seeing relationships between dissimilar things because of how they organize their thoughts.

While growing up, I remember my mother telling a story, and just as she launched into the details, my father would ask, "What's the bottom line?" My mother would get aggravated because she loved to tell stories. My father would be frustrated because he had a hard time making sense of a story without first understanding its point. If only she had known that people have different direction styles, she might have had more opportunities to tell her stories by offering a glimpse of the outcome before she began to share the details.

Tips for Linear Learners

These tips will help you get to the details.

Ask questions. Try to uncover details, facts, and examples that will be helpful to you by asking "Where does this fit?" "When is this likely to happen?" and "How have we gotten to this stage?"

Be patient. Some people prefer less details and fewer facts than you. Help them by offering a quick summary or an overview.

Use your time wisely. Take time to reason things out and break ideas down into smaller pieces, but be mindful of deadlines. Don't let your need for details distract you.

Look for detailed instructions. When possible, request sequential instructions to achieve specific, detailed objectives. When instructions aren't available, create your own, and then follow them.

Stay on track. When people ask you a seemingly unrelated question or make a tangential statement, ask them how it relates or whether they intended to change the subject.

Tips for Working with Linear Learners

If you work with a linear learner, these tips can help you convey the finer points of your message.

Provide details. Be patient when working with people who ask for facts and details. They need these to learn. Provide all the details and facts you can.

Uncover your order. Outline the sequence of topics you'll convey. Explain your process and the approach you'll take, making the organization explicit and clear.

Create transitions. Be cautious not to switch topics too fast. When you make connections between divergent topics, provide transitions and segues.

Explain what's required. Linear learners like to know what will be required of them at the outset. What do they need to know? What should they bring? What will they do first? What will happen at each succeeding step?

State your objectives. When you have objectives and outcomes in mind, spell them out in concrete terms. For example, "By Monday morning, I need the twenty-page report. It should include an executive summary, a complete index, and a glossary of terms. How you organize the body of the text is up to you."

Because global and linear learning styles can run so counter to one another, in groups I encourage people to introduce anything new with a glimpse of the global bird's eye perspective. Linear learners typically have the patience to listen, and global learners need that view to move on.

5

Attend and Observe

Two dogs walk along. One says to the other, "It's always 'sit, stay, heel,' never 'think, create, be aware.'"

Imagine you're driving down the road, with the radio playing; rain is falling, and your children are in the back seat with their seatbelts fastened. Suddenly, the rain turns into a rainstorm and the traffic in front of you begins to pile up. What do you do first? Turn on the windshield wipers. What's the next thing you do? Turn off the radio. You might think you're the only person in the world who does this, but you're not. What is the reason you do it? Attention.

When the weather changed, you went from attending to a few things to facing more than you could handle. You started, without even thinking about it, to lighten your load.

Attention is one of your most important and scarce resources. You can't learn what you can't pay attention to. When everything requires the same type and quantity of attention, it's easy to feel distracted and overwhelmed. This chapter addresses how attention can help you learn more. You'll also have an opportunity to pump up your focus and slow down your habits of perception so that you can become aware of how your attention and observations influence what you can learn.

Road Map to This Chapter

Chapter 5 takes you to the following destinations:

▶ Activating your attention

▶ Multitasking

▶ Avoiding becoming overwhelmed

▶ Focusing exercises

▶ Identifying your observation style

Activate Your Attention

> The range of what we think and do is limited by what we fail to notice. And because we fail to notice that we fail to notice, there is little we can do to change until we notice how failing to notice shapes our thoughts and deeds.
>
> —*Ronald D. Laing*

> It is wise to get knowledge and learning from every source—from a sot, a pot, a fool, a winter-mitten, or an old slipper.
>
> —*Rabelais*

Each of us can pay attention to only a fixed number of senses, thoughts, and emotions at one time. We couldn't possibly manage all that takes place on every level simultaneously, so our awareness focuses on a limited number of things. When you concentrate on a book, noises in the environment fade from consciousness; when your thoughts wander in a conversation, you find yourself unable to recall everything the speaker said, although you were aware that someone was talking to you.

Why do some things catch your attention and other things float by unnoticed? That's because your attention acts sort of like a magazine editor. Editors decide which stories get headlines on the cover, get a prime location in a spot where the magazine opens, or wind up hidden in the back.

This editing and attending begin when you're very young. When a baby starts to develop, it begins to pay attention to light, then voices, and then more external, as well as internal, stimuli. Because we each experience different things, every child becomes an individual, with a unique identity, based on what he or she attends to. In other words, nature (the cells and the physiology we're born with) plus nurture and attention (what we notice during our experiences) lead to who we are and our individual styles. What catches our attention is what we hold in our thoughts, which begins to form a pathway.

Has this ever happened to you? Once you decided to buy a new car, all of a sudden you start to see more of that car model on the streets. Maybe you wonder if they were always there and you just didn't pay attention to them. If the car example doesn't fit, maybe you decided to buy a shirt in an unusual color, and then it seems like everyone is wearing that color of shirt. Women who are trying to become pregnant report that they start to notice pregnant women everywhere they go. The same is true of men who begin to lose their hair. All of these examples relate to what draws your attention and the new pathways that focus has created.

Imagine looking for a specific book on a cluttered shelf. Even though you're bombarded with visual information—stray papers, other books, maybe an odd knickknack or a picture of your last vacation, you find the book amid the clutter because a pathway ignores everything except the book it wants. The shape, size, color, and title of that book are unique compared to the pictures, the shelf itself, and the features of the other books. It's unique because of it font size, shape, and color. Once this pathway senses the object, your attention allows you to see it.

When you're awake, you make an important decision every single moment: You decide where to turn your attention. Most people make this decision about 100,000 times a day.

You're always paying attention to something because your survival depends on it. The attention process consists of an alarm (oooh!), orientation (where?), identification (where is it?), and a decision, to determine how long you should attend to it.

Most people can manipulate their own attention, just as a lighting technician can direct a powerful spotlight beam onto different characters on a theater stage. When you turn your attention beam onto something, you begin to think about it and have the ability to learn from it. Objects outside the periphery lose their distinguishing features and fall out of focus, but, to some degree, you may still be aware of what's happening on the fringe.

It's not that activities on the periphery are fuzzy. They just aren't commanding your direct attention.

How do you swing your attention spotlight from one object or thought to the next? Here are ten tips on activating attention.

1. *Layer.* If you want to solve a problem, keep it at the top of your thoughts. Think about it, talk about it, write about it, and imagine what it will be like when it's complete. I do this whenever possible. During the time period that I wrote this book, I read a novel where the main character studied the body-mind problem and a nonfiction book on brain cancer therapies, did sit ups, practiced yoga, talked about learning with my family, and asked questions of everyone I met.

2. *Try not to repeat yourself.* Whenever you say something so frequently that it becomes routine, your thoughts no longer attend to it. Telling your son to "Sit down, and be quiet" will grab his attention a few times, and he may even comply for a while, but if you begin every meal with that directive, he's likely to not even hear you. After a while he'll have literally tuned you out. Something similar happens when you repeatedly announce the same information. When you tell your children that they get to spend their holiday vacation driving around the state with their parents, their eyes may glaze over if this is the third year in a row you've tried to delight them with this news. Mundane things aren't great attention getters. Try instead to make your announcement special and newsworthy.

3. *Make it novel and rewarding.* You're likely to pay attention to whatever is unique and take note of what's new. This even happens as animals learn. When I write, our schipperke dog spends time with me, on our porch. Usually she lies on the cool ground, sleeps in the fresh air, or wants me to play catch. In the spring and the summer, in particular, little blue lizards make an appearance, running up and down the outside brick wall. Even if the dog seems to be asleep, though, it takes only an instant for her attention to focus on a lizard,

and her whole body springs into motion. Once the lizard gets away, the dog is vigilant for a few minutes, then returns to her restful state. She's able to focus completely when she needs to, but her attention doesn't stay there when the need is gone.

4. *Mix it up.* You may notice that food tends to lose its flavor as you progress through a meal. Even the fifth dip into the jalapeño salsa is always less dramatic than the first. When you experience something new, you take notice and either welcome it or become wary of it. When the same prompt is presented continuously for a long time, your senses believe the signal is routine so your attention moves elsewhere. With food, it takes about one minute of thrilling any one taste receptor for it to reach its sensitivity limit. After that, tastes fade. The best way to circumvent this and to hold your attention is to eat different foods during a meal. Instead of eating all of your chicken at once, mix in some potatoes, some tomatoes, then some green vegetables. When you return to your chicken, your taste buds will attend to it all over again, and it will seem to taste more flavorful.

5. *Recency and primacy.* The tendency to attend to and remember first impressions is known as the *primacy effect.* The tendency to remember the last thing is called the *recency effect.* The recency effect allows you to remember best what you learned last. The primacy effect helps you to remember what you learned first. If you want to keep your attention at its peak, create many beginnings and ends in what you're doing. This may involve stopping frequently and taking breaks, or looking for a new perspective on a regular basis.

6. *Make it silly.* Most people invest too much energy ensuring that they don't look foolish or goofy. Many people have practiced being so cool in every respect that even when they're alone, they're unable to try something new that might make them look or feel silly. To hold your attention, create new pathways, make connections, and find new associations, you should be willing to explore goofy, silly, and even seemingly foolish ideas. If you're not ready to do this in public, try it privately as often as you can. Promise yourself to do at least one silly thing each day. At first, it can be as mundane as brushing your teeth while sitting on the bathroom floor. You might be surprised at what you learn from that perspective. Next, consider making a

funny face at a child, and then at an adult. If you try skipping through a parking lot or walking backward down a hall, you'll find yourself paying attention to very different sensations.

7. ***Don't get overwhelmed.*** Have you ever decided to clean the attic, but, after rummaging through it, you decided to work in the garden instead? How about committing to write a big report, but once you looked though all of the information, you suddenly remembered that a smaller project was overdue? These types of situations happen to all of us and are examples of overloaded attention. Despite your good intentions of cleaning up or preparing to begin a project, you gave up before you started. The tasks were so large, you didn't know where to begin. Were you attentive? Yes, but you were so overstimulated that you couldn't attend anymore. You might even have felt like your attention overwhelmed your body. You became tired ("I'll clean the attic after a nap") or even sick ("The thought of writing that report made me queasy"). To avoid shutting down from "overwhelm," break a daunting project into several smaller steps; then attend to one step at a time.

8. ***Find a common theme.*** If you're feeling overwhelmed by the myriad of different tasks you need to complete today or how different the people you're working with seem to be, think about how each project or errand you work on is similar to the other things you're working on, how they all relate, or what lessons they might share. Then, when you're focused on any one, you can leverage what you're learning and see if it might offer you some insight into doing something else.

9. ***Simplify.*** Sometimes your desire to cover all the bases, respond to each opportunity, or provide every possible option can frazzle your attention. But what if you just had less to focus on? Oh, don't laugh so hard at me! Right at the point when I thought I had it all, I realized that I had no time to attend to any of it. So, I devoted the little time I had (which I previously would cram with extra projects) to de-stuff, de-schedule, and de-stuff some more. Even though I couldn't keep every distraction off my path, just having less stuff around, fewer choices in my life, and less on my plate allowed me to finally focus on what mattered most. If I could do it, so can you.

10. *Ask for assistance.* Sometimes all the strategies you can muster won't help you solve a problem that you just can't see through without help. For instance, I used to misplace my keys at least once a week. Then one day my husband asked, "Why don't you always put them in the same place when you come home?" and I wondered, "Why didn't I think of that?" It sounded so basic, but no matter how motivated I was to find my keys, I would not have found that solution. It's easy to forget that other people are usually available and very interested in directing your attention, offering suggestions, and providing knowledge, guidance, emotional support, comfort, or even physical aid when you try to learn something new. Only by asking can you learn from them and with them. When you ask, you connect with someone who can help you learn.

Improve Your Awareness

Ask yourself, "What am I paying attention to right now?" Maybe you're thinking about what will happen in the next few minutes, about an appointment you have tomorrow, or about something that has already happened.

Then ask, "What am I sensing?" Possibly you're thinking about the feel of the book in your hand, the hum of the light above you, the whistle of a bird, or the TV playing in the next room?

Observe yourself at this very moment. Be aware of what your inner observer encourages you to notice or drops on a moment-by-moment basis.

To get in the habit of watching your attention, copy the following list to a separate piece of paper, and post it somewhere so that you can look at the questions each day.

- ▶ What am I doing right now?
- ▶ What am I thinking about right now?
- ▶ What *else* am I thinking about now?
- ▶ What have I learned?
- ▶ What works for me?

▶ What's my body telling me?

▶ What will I be introduced to today?

▶ Will I be open enough to see it?

If you're not aware of what you're doing at the time you do it, you may miss an opportunity to learn from each moment.

Multitasking

> This above all; to thine own self be true.
>
> —*William Shakespeare*

Even though it may seem like you're juggling a dozen activities and multitasking every minute of the day, it only feels that way. You're really darting back and forth between several tasks, holding only one in full focus at any given time. You're switching your attention quickly back and forth.

The number of tasks you feel as if you can pay attention to depends upon the difficulty of the tasks. A well-learned task, such as walking, takes little effort and doesn't impede how you perform another task.

A more difficult task, like walking backwards uphill, requires more concentration and may completely impede your efforts to hold a conversation. When actions are familiar, you can likely do two or even three of them.

When tasks are less automatic, as with a friend of mine who tries to read four web sites, compose an e-mail, and talk on the telephone at the same time, you'll find yourself aware that you're jumping back and forth, and you're probably not gaining any real time. The same will hold true for you with any two activities when one of them challenges you or requires some level of focus.

A quick way to picture this is to compare multitasking to the number of burners on a stove. You can have pots on five burners at the same time if they have regular stirring cycles, but only two pots (maybe three) if they are big or require constant attention.

How Many Tasks Can You Attend to at Once?

Ask yourself this: How many things are you aware that you are attending to when you hit that turn-off-the-radio stage, when you reach your maximum capacity to multitask? By reflecting on that number, you can discover whether you're a many-burners person or someone who needs to have fewer activities going—whether you can multitask many things or you know that you ought to focus on one thing at a time. The caveat to figuring out your number is to recognize that some things take all of your attention, and physical things, in many cases, take more than one *type* of attention. Sometimes tasks require smell, other times touch, and often they require many different senses at once.

Think about the number of things you can attend to seemingly simultaneously. The maximum is usually about seven. Most people say that for them, it's comfortably two or three. This is how many things they can actively work on at some level—that is, both physically and mentally. Beyond that, they need to start backing out of one or more activities.

When someone asks you to take on something new, consider replying, "What can you take off my plate in exchange?" It's helpful to get in the habit of figuring out how you can minimize what you need to pay attention to before you try to add on anything more.

When you see people talking on cell phones while driving or walking down the street, do you ever wonder how much they're learning from the person they're talking to? I usually guess that they aren't learning much. Although there is some opportunity for learning over a cell phone, trying to learn while you talk, drive, and work isn't usually a good idea. With each task you pay attention to, you diminish your overall ability to do any one.

Another attention metaphor is that of juggling. Some people can juggle two balls, some three, some four, and some people can juggle even more. Ask real jugglers and they'll tell you that after three, you need to learn a pattern.

An intriguing aspect of the juggling metaphor is to consider how you juggle two kinds of balls: rubber balls and glass balls. Rubber balls could represent community and work activities. If you drop a rubber ball, it bounces right back and you don't even have to reach for it. Glass balls represent your family, your friends, and your health, and they don't bounce. They chip and may even shatter.

Until you learn how many things you can reasonably attend to—and which activities require your full attention—you will struggle with learning more of anything right now.

Focus Your Attention

> Being properly distracted for a moment is child's play.
> Being rightly distracted for a lifetime is an art.
>
> —*Douglas Adams*

> Methinks that the moment my legs begin to move, my thoughts begin to flow.
>
> —*Henry David Thoreau*

Here are several activities you can use to focus your attention and increase your ability to observe the world around you, because, in effect, you can quiet your distractions.

Move Your Hands

You might find it easier to focus on listening to something, reading a story, or even talking when you can move your hands around.

Silly Putty or a spongy toy can prove quite useful to hold and play with as you learn. In my workshops, I place these toys on tables around the room and I always have some sort of toy on my desk. If you try this, too, you might notice that you play without even noticing, and you may find that when your hands are involved, you learn more effectively.

Centering

Finding a calm place inside yourself helps you relax and increases your awareness. It's especially helpful to engage your whole body in order to narrow your focus. I learned these exercises during a yoga class with busy executives interested in improving their ability to concentrate on the job and moms improving their stamina. Even though you may find the practices awkward at first, after you go through this routine several times, you'll discover that it offers a fabulous stretch and will help you focus on whatever you want to learn.

1. ***Count your breaths.*** Sit in a relaxed position and take a few deep breaths. Bring your attention to your breathing and notice each time

you breathe in and out. Silently count each exhalation up to a count of ten. If you lose count, just start over at one. Repeat this process for five minutes.

2. *Body awareness.* Sit in a relaxed position and take a few deep breaths. Bring your attention to any part of your body. Inhale deeply into that area, letting it relax on the exhalation. Continue this process for five minutes. If your attention wanders, just bring your attention back to the body part and continue.

3. *Move your focus up.* Sit in a relaxed position and take a few deep breaths. Inhaling, raise your right arm, and pause. Exhaling, turn your head to the left and bring your right hand to your collarbone, then pause. With your right hand, massage under your collarbone, at both sides of the breastbone, and pause. Then slowly inhale. Exhaling, slowly turn your head to the center and bring your left hand to your mouth, and pause. While massaging your collarbone with your right hand, rub above and below the lips with your left hand. Breathing slowly in and out, continue to massage these two places for a slow and gentle count of ten. Inhaling, slowly bring your arms back to your sides.

Untangle Your Thinking

This activity is especially helpful when you find it difficult to think and do something at the same time. It's sort of like marching but with a twist. I learned this activity from a physical therapist who found that it helped her clients coordinate their activities in new and powerful ways.

1. March slowly in place (or around, if you're in a large space). As your right knee comes up, use your left hand to touch that knee. With the next set, touch your right hand to your left knee. Move your opposite arm and leg very deliberately and slowly. Alternate sides ten times.

2. Then, switch to a one-sided march, with the same-sided hand and leg moving together, like a marionette on a string, yet also very deliberately and slowly. Alternate sides ten times.

3. Return to the alternate side march and do that ten times.

Pheromones of Learning

From our birth to the grave, the joys of odors
enrich and mold our days and our lives with powerful
memories.

—James Kohl

Sometimes you learn about attention in the oddest of circumstances.

One summer, I facilitated a workshop in Minneapolis on complexity theory. The participants were some of the most brilliant people I had ever met. At one point, everyone went outside to move around and work together in small groups, wrestling with the specific issues of their organizations.

I walked into the hallway to visit the water fountain and stretch a little, too. When I came back into the room, empty of people but full of wild models people had built out of Zome tools on their tables, I was almost knocked over by a force I couldn't identify but that was as real and powerful as a crowd at a NASCAR race. It was intoxicating, energizing, and stunning. It felt both familiar and unusual, and it held me, almost buzzing, in the room for a few minutes.

When I wandered outside, I sat with one of the groups and I explained what had just happened. One of the workshop participants, a scientist, looked me square in the face and said, "That's the 'pheromones of learning.' Didn't you feel it when we were all in there? It was palpable." He explained that pheromones are working all around us, helping to focus our thoughts and directing our attention all the time.

Scientists have long known that odors and subliminal scents, *pheromones*, influence how animals develop, bond, and nurture their offspring. Recently, they've discovered that human animals are no exception. Pheromones influence how the brain develops, what you remember, and how you learn. Odors provide a completely new way of thinking about learning, and it's right under your nose.

So what about the pheromones of learning? Humans emit pheromones in all bodily fluids, including perspiration. And what better way to work up a healthy sweat than by learning? Maybe our call to learn together is governed by much more than motivation. Some behavior may be subtly affected by chemicals secreted by our peers.

Organize Your Observations

> The events in our lives happen in a sequence in
> time, but in their significance to ourselves they find
> their own order . . . the continuous thread of
> revelation.
>
> *—Eudora Welty*

How you organize your observations also plays a big role in how you learn. Consider this example.

I'm on the board of an international organization with people who never seem able to make decisions. When we met together in person for the first time, it became clear that part of the problem was that our attention styles were very different. A handful of board members carefully prepared our schedule before we arrived, so that once we were together, we could get started. Within the first hour of our meeting, however, two board members began discussing how the layout of the room didn't suit them. Another two shared long tales of how they'd faced similar situations in the past, and another board member invariably challenged any topic proposed for decision. The facilitator became frustrated because the agenda, and the decisions on which his day-to-day work depended, had been abandoned.

Over dinner, a small group asked if I might have an idea of what went wrong. At first it looked like a clash of personalities, but the more time we spent together, the more I began to notice it was something more fundamental. We each focused on and paid attention to very different things.

Sound familiar? Maybe our dynamics were similar to those you face in meetings or with your family. Resolving problems like these can begin when you recognize that the issue may be less personality driven than attention driven—and that this is easier to address than you might realize.

These attention styles are based on your preference for structuring thoughts, according to one of four simple patterns. I haven't provided an assessment quiz here, because I find that most people can figure out their style by reading through the options. You also probably will find it easy to spot these styles in your friends, family members, or coworkers.

What's Your Attention Style?

Each of us has adopted habits of ordering what holds our attention by time, space, comparison, or contradiction. Although we use all four, most of us rely on one style more than on the others.

If you're *time-oriented*, you may reveal your preference for organizing by making lists and prioritizing them in a certain order. Other people may notice that you recount stories or begin an agenda by saying, "First we'll do this . . . and then . . . and then . . ."

If you're *space-oriented*, you may prefer to order items by making a place for them and may understand ideas by breaking them into categories. You may illustrate your ideas with flow charts or mind maps, and people around you may notice this style by observing how attentive you are to making the space around you feel right and by seeing how meticulously you organize your kitchen, closets, desk, shelves, or office.

If you're *comparison-oriented*, you may reveal your prevailing pattern by likening each idea or situation you meet to another you previously witnessed. You may be an avid storyteller, hearing information by comparing it to what you've experienced before. Other people may hear you relate everything that is said to something else in your life.

If you're *contradiction-oriented*, you may confront new information by challenging it. You may be a skillful debater who makes sense of ideas by contrasting them against their opposite. People may perceive you as being negative or contrary, even though you're only seeking a clear distinction and an understanding of what something is not.

Let's look at each of these styles in more detail.

Are You a Time Learner?

I've had a wonderful time, but this wasn't it.

—*Groucho Marx*

Time-oriented learners reveal their preference by making lists and turning them into priorities, then schedules. When asked to explain something to other people, they itemize points and assign these items an order.

They are likely to keep all their scheduled appointments and complete all the tasks on their lists. You can easily recognize someone is time-oriented because they almost count out the minutes with words such as, "when . . ." and "then, and then, and then . . ."

As I was growing up, my dad often exclaimed, "Make a list!" followed by his favorite question, "Have you made a list?" In our house, there were stacks of notepaper on every flat surface, usually with a few worn-down pencils beside them, in anticipation of a conversation about making a list. No topic was too philosophical, no plan too small to squeak by without the request for a list. This was the same man who was late to everything in his life, who couldn't guess how long anything took, and who didn't go in to work on any day before 10 A.M. Yet he never went to bed without finishing everything he had to do or without knowing what needed to come first, second, and third. His thoughts might not have been on time, but they were about time.

Are You a Space Learner?

Space is the breath of art.

—*Frank Lloyd Wright*

Space-oriented learners pay attention to the order of things by finding a place for them. They categorize ideas and break overwhelming concepts into manageable parts. Rather than writing lists, they illustrate their thoughts with flow charts, maps, and pictures. In their environment, everything is categorized carefully and in its proper place.

My friend Campbell and I attended a fundraiser held in an old theater lobby. Acoustics were awful and the food was mediocre, but the causes were heartwarming. The fact no one could hear anyone else talk (let alone the people onstage raffling items) seemed not to bother anyone but Campbell. He was about to have a conniption. "The space," he said (repeatedly), as he waved his arms around butterfly style, "is all wrong! These causes are too important for this to be messed up." He walked around, looking at the partitions in the room, the lights, the way the fabric draped over the tables, and anything with an impact on the atmosphere. He didn't care that almost no one else at the event had any issue with the space. For him, it felt awkward and required his attention.

Barbara, an artist living in a house that overlooks the ocean in rural Nova Scotia, is the mother of two, a nine-year-old boy and a twelve-year-old girl; she's a cook, a chauffeur, a housekeeper, a gardener, and a tutor. Along with being an artist and a parent, she has been dedicated to a meditation practice for twenty years. She understands that she achieves balance and perspective by allowing herself basic space. When I visited her home, I was awed not only by the beauty of their homestead and her breathtaking artwork, which also included furniture and sculptures, but by the sense of space that she created throughout and around the house. It felt like a space where anyone could learn anything. The next day, when I joined her and her son for breakfast, and the conversation turned to his wide-ranging taste in music, the breadth of his interests, and the curiosity that practically oozed out of his pores, I could see that she'd help to foster that space within her son as well. He believes that he can learn and do anything, and I have no doubt that he can.

Are You a Comparison Learner?

The caterpillar's new cells are called imaginal cells. They resonate at a different frequency. . . . A long string of clumping and clustering imaginal cells, all resonating at the same frequency, all passing information from one to another there inside the chrysalis. Then at some point, the entire long string of imaginal cells suddenly realizes all together that it is something different from the caterpillar. Happy birthday butterfly!

—*Nori Huddle*

Comparison-oriented learners connect each idea or situation they encounter to another situation they've already experienced. If you listen carefully to their stories, you can hear that they absorb and order information by comparing and fitting it into their thoughts about what they've experienced before. They highlight or illustrate any point they're trying to make with descriptions of people they know, or a sequence of examples pulled from something they've seen or heard.

Sandra, a marketing director at a university, compares each of her experiences with something she's done before, in stories that almost seem too amazing to be true. She told me about her adventures when she taught a remedial writing class for incoming college students, worked for a business journal, and grew her school's new container-plant distance learning program. This was her way to describe organizing styles and to organize her own attention by making the information real to her, and attending to the topics as we talked.

Howard, somewhat of a modern-day renaissance man, uses analogies that frequently relate to technology, architecture, world-class toys, or fine woodworking. If you talked with him long enough, you'd begin to believe that everything in life is like a prefabricated building part, a LEGO toy, a cabinet, or a handheld computer. Frequently, it requires getting to the end of his story to understand the relationship between one thing and the other, but the connection is always there. His comparisons are like a complicated game, requiring you to open all the doors to reveal what's inside.

Are You a Contradiction Learner?

I put forward at once—lest I break with my style, which is affirmative and deals with contradiction and criticism only as a means, only involuntarily—the three tasks for which educators are required. One must learn to see, one must learn to think, one must learn to speak and write: the goal in all three is a noble culture.

—*Friedrich Nietzsche*

Contradiction-oriented learners confront new information by challenging it. They're prone to debate, and, as you observe them, you can see they pay attention to what *something is not*. For example, they may say, "We can't get started next week. When can we get started?" or "I don't like the way that sounds; how about this instead?"

My neighbor developed all of the symptoms that I had from lactose intolerance. As she rattled off how she felt, I encouraged her to replace her regular milk with acidophilus milk for a week and see if her symptoms changed. "Oh, that isn't it," she replied. "I can't have that. I know it." When I asked why, she had an arsenal of reasons at her disposal—as with so many conversations we've had over the years. Eventually, after she has disagreed long enough, she'll begin to consider what I proposed. This usually happens only when it doesn't contradict whatever viewpoint she first argued for. It takes time, but she gets there. She isn't being disagreeable or even contrary, but until she first looks at something from the opposing angle, she can't find a place for it in her own thoughts or find a way to take it under consideration.

Gordon, an educator, does something similar, although he'd argue persuasively that he doesn't. No matter what the suggestion, the question, the idea, or the thought, he plays devil's advocate. He takes on this role to give himself time to look at the opposing perspectives, which helps him to understand for himself what he thinks. It's a fascinating angle: looking at something from its negative in order for the picture to be revealed.

Working with Various Styles

No one pays attention with just one of these styles. You probably use a variety of them as you talk, listen, and think something through. So do the people around you.

Knowing that these differences can arise in a group can help you recognize another person's pressure points. For example, time and space learners are often impatient with comparison and contradiction learners' lack of straightforward thought. Comparison learners, in particular, might find time and space learners too rigid and too impatient. Contradiction learners may panic everyone else by picking apart a good idea, and comparison learners can take an idea on frequent side journeys, as well as into extenuating circumstances they feel compelled to share.

If you can recognize differences in these four modes and can begin to notice how they influence the way you organize your thoughts (and what you say about those thoughts), you can learn to appreciate them and address them in a diplomatic and nonjudgmental way if they become problems.

For instance, instead of saying, "You're getting us sidetracked," try, "Let's look at an example before we begin." Instead of, "Why do you take a negative approach?" try, "Let's look at this from another angle." As you become more familiar with your own style, you'll find it much easier to discover a way to see other people's styles and to pay attention to how you can complement each other's work. You'll find that comparison and contradiction learners are great at providing analysis. Time and space thinkers are great organizers and doers once the decision is made.

6

Mind Your Gaps

I am struck once again by the unutterable beauty, terror, and strangeness of everything we think we know.

— *Edward Abbey*

Be who you are and say what you feel, because those who mind don't matter and those who matter don't mind.

— *Theodore Geisel (Dr. Seuss)*

Sometimes what you need to learn may be obvious. For instance, you know in advance that if you want to be able to speak brilliantly in front of a group, you need confidence, as well as speaking, presentation, and communication skills. Yet at other times, you might not discover your shortcomings until you begin something new. Halfway through voicing your opinion at a community meeting, you may discover that you also need the skill to answer questions in public without having time to prepare. Suddenly you realize that you don't have a clue how to proceed or you lack a necessary periphery skill, like answering tough questions, and it might not have occurred to you that you need this skill until the moment you realize you don't have it.

Learning can be subtle—so subtle that sometimes it's difficult for us to figure out how we learn. We just do.

This chapter explains how you can pursue what you don't know—in an organized way, without limiting yourself—in order to learn more about almost any topic and adjust for new experiences that come along. If you recognize the holes in your knowledge and understanding, you can then identify effective ways to fill the gaps and can work through what else you need to learn.

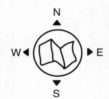

Road Map to This Chapter

Chapter 6 takes you to the following destinations:

▶ Taking inventory of what you know

▶ Working through the learning process

▶ Examining what you know

▶ Asking big questions

▶ Creating serendipity in your life

Take Inventory

> There is something I don't know, that I am supposed to know. I don't know what it is I don't know, and yet am supposed to know, and I feel I look stupid if I seem both not to know it and not to know what it is I don't know. Therefore, I pretend to know it. This is nerve-wracking since I don't know what I must pretend to know. Therefore, I pretend I know everything.
>
> —*Ronald D. Laing*

Wherever you recognize gaps in your knowledge, similar to when you notice a missing piece in a jigsaw puzzle or a hole in a piece of Swiss cheese, it's helpful to look at what *is* there before trying to fill in what's missing.

One way that I determine how I'll approach learning something new is to ask myself and reflect on the following questions.

What am I trying to do?

What do I want to learn?

What do I need to learn to accomplish what I'm trying to do?

What else will I get, in addition to learning this?

What capabilities do I have right now?

What competencies am I interested in developing?

What structures and practices am I willing to set up to help me develop new competencies?

The Swiss-Cheese Model

Self-knowledge is probably the most important
thing in becoming a champion.

—Billy Jean King

I use a Swiss cheese image to help recognize the stage where I am in my
own learning. You may also find it helpful for yourself or when you learn
with other people.

When you're new to something, you have many holes in what you
know. You probably have more holes in what you know than you have
understanding. If you can begin to fill one of those gaping holes, you feel
as if you've made real progress. That's why none of us expects to pick up
a new language we know nothing about very quickly. We recognize that
we have plenty to learn, and proceed accordingly.

When you've progressed to an intermediate level, you have fewer
holes, but you begin to expect that you should understand and you may
become impatient with how long the learning process can take.

When you become an expert in something, you still have holes in your
understanding, but not that many. At this point, your impatience levels
off, and when you fill even one hole, you probably become excited. After
all, learning something new doesn't happen all that often when you're an
expert.

Look at the cheese picture, then turn back to the previous series of
questions. Assess your stage: big holes, midsize, or small.

Know, Do, and Feel

Speak your mind, even when your voice shakes.

—Maggie Kuhn

Select a fairly straight-forward skill you'd like to improve, such as your
performance as a speaker, swimmer, golfer, gardener, or cook.

Then ask yourself, "What do I need to know, do, and believe to feel
like I've improved in this?" In other words, what working knowledge,
practical skills, and authentic attitudes do you require to succeed?

For example, in the case of speaking in public, the elements might look like this:

Working Knowledge	**Practical Skills**	**Authentic Attitudes**
I would need to know something special about the subject.	I would need the skills to express my ideas simply, at the right pace, and with the right emphasis.	I would need confidence and a relaxed attitude.
I would need to know the vocabulary used in the subject I want to speak about.	I would need to be able to organize my presentation logically, include interesting facts, and use great looking illustrations.	I would need to truly care about the subject, and believe the people listening to me would benefit from the information I'm presenting.

Use this space to write down the knowledge, skills, and attitudes you'd need, in order to feel as if you've taken on something important. Check your list with other people who have mastered this same topic, to get their perspective on your approach. *Golfer*

Working Knowledge	**Practical Skills**	**Authentic Attitudes**
Fundamentals	*To hit the ball Straight*	*Patience*
Rules		*Confidence*
Techniques	*Putt*	
Hold Club		

Why is attitude important? Your self-image, including your beliefs about what you are and aren't capable of, is linked to your emotions, what you pay attention to, and, therefore, what you can learn. If someone persuades you that you're unlikely to learn or be able to do something or that you're "not that kind of person," you might find it impossible to move forward because you'll be directing your attention elsewhere, and may make an entire skill inaccessible. If, however, you break down what you need into these three areas, you'll be able to hold your attention and work through each activity until you feel ready.

What Do You Know?

> Not everything that can be counted counts, and not everything that counts can be counted.
>
> —*Albert Einstein*

The word *test* draws gut-level memories of difficult times in school-like settings when I felt unprepared or manipulated to learn something that didn't seem very important. Magnify that by the average number of quizzes that most students face before they're eighteen years old (2,500), and you might be surprised to find me writing about testing here.

It's sad that the word *testing* has such a bad rap, though. Most of us, beginning in childhood, have an intrinsic ability to test our own progress and should consider the value of testing to help us learn more. Maybe we should call it "finding out how much we know" instead of "test"?

Testing is a natural aspect of your ability to learn. It should be a simple validation that what you've learned is what you ought to have learned, showing that you've progressed from being a novice to something more— sometimes an expert, other times just knowing enough to proceed.

If you want to find out how well you know something, try this simple test.

Level 1: Do I know enough so that I can think about it? Do I grasp the subject and some of the related issues?

Level 2: Do I know enough to talk about it? Can I name some examples and similar ideas?

Level 3: Do I know enough to teach it? Can I explain the important characteristics to someone else?

Level 4: Do I know enough to debate the issues? Can I work though the subject if I'm challenged on certain points?

Discover your level of understanding by periodically asking yourself:

What do I know?

How do I know it?

Which aspects am I unsure about?

What can I do to develop a more complete understanding?

Where can I learn more?

What can I do to strengthen and challenge what I think I understand?

The Learning Process

> The road to wisdom?—Well, it's plain
> and simple to express:
> Err
> and err
> and err again
> but less
> and less
> and less.
>
> —*Piet Hein*

Learning occurs in six interlinked stages—inviting, sensing, synthesizing, reflecting, ruminating, acting—and then beginning again. These elements can be integrated together and can happen fast. Even though you don't need to complete all the steps to learn, the more stages you work through, the greater your transformation.

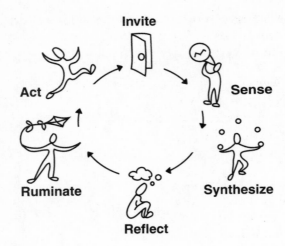

Inviting immerses you initially so that you can begin to make sense of something. It's your motivation, what draws you to learn. Because learning begins with a pull, inviting is a prerequisite to any further learning. If you weren't prompted to learn something (from either a force within you or being coerced by external forces), you'd never begin to learn.

Sensing simply means gathering information through your senses. This can be from a lecture, a picture, a meal, or a dance. Your preferred learning styles will guide how you take in information most effectively.

Synthesis occurs as you internalize the new information and check it against what you already know, from facts, opinions, beliefs, values, thoughts, and memories. As you begin to add and test, organize and integrate, you match the new information with your prior knowledge, making connections and associations, and accepting or rejecting what you're taking in. In other words, when you find a place for what you learn, you can begin to comprehend it.

Reflecting ensues when you contemplate and connect how what you're learning influences some aspect of your life and you consider whether your learning might offer a new way for you to behave. When you reflect, you can also look at what other peo-

ple say, what other people have done, and where what you learn
fits into your situation. You may even make a few predictions and
think about how what you're learning could change your life.

Ruminating comes about when you let what you're learning be
with you, letting it stir around in your subconscious. You don't
directly think about it but rather just let it be. This process can
help you fill in gaps that linear or focused thinking just can't do.
It also provides a chance to recognize interconnections.

Acting takes place when you begin to use what you've learned
to complete a task, solve a problem, or do something new. You
interact with what you've learned, use it, enhance it, and
become improved by it. You can now express or apply what
you've learned because your capacity to act has changed and
something inside of you, at a cellular level, has adjusted.

You could compare the learning process to cooking. Imagine yourself
baking bread, for instance. You begin with a reason to make the bread.
Maybe you want to sell it at a fair or make it for your family (invitation).
Then you move the ingredients (sense) into a bowl and mix them
together (synthesis). As the elements—yeast, flour, and heat—act on each
other, they change (reflect). As the dough rises (rumination), it becomes
something entirely different. Finally, you bake the dough, and the bread
is ready to be eaten or stored (act).

Learning Barriers

Various barriers can interrupt the cycle at any stage. If you're invited to
learn something that seems dangerous, that goes against your values, or
you have a hunch it wouldn't help you progress, you might at first be curious to learn, but almost immediately, you walk away or begin to tune out.
It's hard to learn anything that seems boring, holds no meaning for you,
or goes against what you believe. There are also more subtle barriers.

Suppose you're interested in learning something but have difficulty
understanding the words you read; you may have trouble focusing on the
page because of distractions in the room, or you can't find your glasses.

Maybe you're unable to relate the new information to your current knowledge or have difficulty remembering information in sequence. Maybe once you get the gist of something, you realize it just doesn't hold your attention as much as it did when you didn't understand it.

Suppose you're just too busy to spend time thinking about something other than the information, and you would rather let your whole body make connections that your logical brain can't make for you at this time.

Or perhaps you have difficulty expressing what you've learned or finding time to put it into action.

You're likely to act in a certain way (based on your styles, your preferences, and the pathways that past experiences have created), until you find your limits or experience an inability to do something. If you can discover which stage breaks down, you can change strategies and approach the problem area in a new way. When that happens, try different ways until you find one that works. Try to engage your whole body. Then a new pathway or connection will be formed to incorporate the new way into your repertoire of what you can do.

Create Mental Furniture

> Making mental connections is our most critical learning tool, the essence of human intelligence: to forge links; to go beyond the given; to see patterns, relationship, context.
>
> —*Marilyn Ferguson*

> There is always one moment in childhood when the door opens and lets the future in.
>
> —*Graham Greene*

When you're introduced to a new concept, do you ever find that it doesn't seem to land anywhere, it just spins in your thoughts? Maybe you're thinking, "Am I supposed to know what to do next?" Or "What should I do with this? How can I use this?" Perhaps you think about it repeatedly, without the situation improving in any way.

This happens because you don't have the structure for the new information to "sit it down on" in your thoughts. You have nothing to connect it to that you are already familiar with, that you have come to rely on, or have previously made your own. Imagine a house for your thoughts: You don't have a couch where it can rest.

To move past these barriers, it helps to have what I call *mental furniture* formed from experiences, analogies, models, and pathways in your life. It is the base of what you know.

The information that you think about and set down on your mental furniture changes as you learn anything new, as you challenge what you've done in the past, and even during the course of a single conversation. Everything adjusts all the time.

The following exercise can help you become aware of how you use your mental furniture.

For a few minutes, close your eyes and imagine yourself walking through a house that doesn't have any furniture or other people in it. Picture yourself walking around, looking around, and doing whatever you'd like to do. Enjoy yourself.

Open your eyes and write out what you did. *Looked @ how I would Set up each room, Setup my own personale Room, Big Screen TV System*

Now, imagine that people are in the house with you, but there is still no furniture. What are you doing differently? How are you interacting with the other people? What are you doing that you wouldn't have done alone?

Then write down what happened. *TAlKing about the different Rooms, Painting, carpet, Bathrooms, features*

Now, imagine the house filled with people and furniture. Again, observe what you do differently. Think about what you're doing.

Write down what you did. *Rearrange things, new ideas what to do*

When I do this exercise with groups, I have heard these sorts of replies.

"When the house was empty, I wandered around wherever I wanted to go. When people appeared, I stopped and talked. When furniture appeared, then I had to plan my path. I had to interact in some way with the furniture and eventually I sat down."

"When the house was empty, I noticed all the space. When there were people, my vision narrowed. Then when there was furniture, my focus narrowed again and I was no longer aware of the space."

"Almost immediately, I dropped to the floor and looked up at the walls and ceiling. How luxurious. When people came in, I felt inhibited to enjoy the area. Then they joined me on the floor, enjoying the view above. When there was furniture to contend with, I felt my freedom inhibited temporarily, but then we started jumping up and down on the sofa."

Examining your own house of thoughts, and how you prefer to furnish it, ought to give you some important clues into how you prefer to build your structures alone and with other people.

Stay Curious

> I think, at a child's birth, if a mother could ask a fairy godmother to endow it with the most useful gift, that gift would be curiosity.
>
> —*Eleanor Roosevelt*

> Knowledge is good, but wonder is priceless. The one is of the mind, the other of the spirit.
>
> —*Virginia Eifert*

All of us come into the world inquisitive, curious about people around us, and interested in exploring new things. From birth—and, some would argue, even before that—our senses are attuned to discovering, experimenting, and learning from everything in our environment. We touch whatever we can, we put everything in our mouths (including our feet!), and we're fascinated by everything that our senses detect.

Parents and teachers sometimes shut down children's natural curiosity when they feel pestered by a constant barrage of questions. Perhaps they are frustrated by not knowing the right answers themselves or they can't appreciate childlike wonder. Many adults find it difficult to say, "I don't know," because they think they *should* know.

With each transition, children's inquisitiveness becomes more cautious and they begin to place value on knowledge rather than inquisitiveness because they get grades and other rewards for the correct answers and for saying and doing things "the right way."

You could almost say that natural interest is trained out of us as we're taught to value the right answer above our inclination to explore. As we grow older, it's easy to become attached to what we know, and soon we find that our natural wonder has diminished. Eventually, many of us become skeptical of any activity we can't immediately justify as leading to a specific, tangible, and actionable result. Even if you did go in search of the right answer or the best solution, you'd discover that there aren't enough precise formulas in the universe to fit every situation you find yourself in; most situations today don't have one perfect answer that will satisfy each gap.

Curiosity is about the value and the power inherent in finding something new to learn in every situation by continuing to imagine and wonder.

I don't mean to imply that factual answers and expert advice aren't valuable. They're tremendously valuable when they help you take action and inquire further. Your value as a learner is not based solely on what you know but also on your ability to be inquisitive. *Not knowing* is your starting point for inquiring, receiving knowledge, and creating new learning.

There are whole families of effective answers, and instead of looking for one right way, we ought to remain curious about a solution with the openness to adjust to the next one, and the one after that.

Although you may feel at times like you've lost that curious urge, I don't know anyone who doesn't secretly use it when no one is looking. You haven't lost your childlike sense of curiosity; it's built upon the same natural impulse that led you to turn the last page. We all have the desire to learn more.

Our challenge is to actively express our inquisitive nature, see opportunities to learn in everything we do, and cultivate the ability and the willingness to risk, to experiment, and to learn from all situations. Enjoy the adventure of discovering how to act when the rules change.

Here are ten things you can do to reignite your sense of curiosity:

1. List in your journal one hundred things you *don't* know.

2. Spend time with a master of a subject you don't know, and practice being curious with this person.

3. Spend time with a child, looking from the child's perspective at the world and the questions he or she asks.

4. Practice not knowing in familiar situations. Notice when you don't know something, and pay attention to where that leads you.

5. Even when you do think you know the answer to something, qualify it with "I think the answer is . . ." followed by, "What do you think?" and see if that elicits an open conversation.

6. Ask people close to you about something you've wondered about them. After they respond, figure out what part of their answer made you genuinely curious, and then ask another question to satisfy that curiosity.

7. Strike up a conversation with someone you don't talk with frequently; ask what he or she has been thinking about recently, and see where the conversation goes.

8. List five things you always wanted to do but never immersed yourself in. Go and do at least one.

9. Identify a second and a third right answer after you think you've found the first right answer.

10. Each morning ask yourself, "What do I wonder about today?"

As you discover more about the world around you, focus your attention on specific areas where you'd like to stretch your knowledge and experience. Focusing your curiosity may lead you to turn your curiosity into a question, and another, and another, which is the basis for learning more.

Create Questions

> It is important that students bring a certain ragamuffin barefoot irreverence to their studies; they are not here to worship what is known, but to question it.
>
> —*Jacob Bronowski*

> Judge a man by his questions rather than his answers.
>
> —*François Marie Arouet, a.k.a. Voltaire*

There are two ways to find answers to what you want to know: You can make assumptions or you can ask questions. Because making assumptions is risky, it's important to learn how to use questions skillfully and to keep yourself open to asking even more.

As soon as children can speak, they start asking questions. At first, it's, "Why is that?" and "What's this?" Soon, they add gigantic questions, such as, "Where does the sky come from?" or "What's weather?"

This breadth of interest and willingness to question everything should never go away, even when we reach adulthood. "Why does this sink leak?" or even the almost-interesting, "Why *isn't* the grass green?" The key is to keep asking these questions with intensity the rest of your life.

Isaac Newton never stopped asking big questions. Even as an adult, he compared himself to a small child on the beach, fascinated with stones and seashells. When people around him couldn't answer his big questions—for instance, "Why is the sky blue?"—he didn't stop asking. In the case of the blue sky, he realized that no one had an answer because the mathematics that might begin to answer the question didn't yet exist. Instead of stopping there, he created calculus. He didn't have the math, so he discovered the math. I wish a teacher had offered that story in math class as a way to encourage my questions.

Nobel Prize–winning physicist Richard Feynman's mother asked her children each day after school, "Did you ask any good questions?" This query connected him and his siblings with what went on in their thoughts and their environment. It also asked them to consider possibilities, pay attention to their curiosity, and cultivate a sense to inquire even more.

There are two types of questions: open questions and closed questions. *Open questions* invite a wide variety of responses; *closed questions* have a single answer. Which do you think evokes more discovery? Open questions.

What are some examples of big open questions? Write down a few here. You'll find that they often begin with words like *what, how, when,* and *where.*

1. who invented football

2. How can we teach mentorship

3. How did you learn to play the guitar

Closed questions limit the response and can be used to lead people in the direction you want them to go, but at a cost. Short replies might leave out important details.

What are some examples of closed questions? They usually begin with words like *have, did, do, would,* or *is.*

1. Did you pick up your clothes

2. Is your name?

3. Do you have a dollar.

How can you sharpen your question-asking skills? Begin by asking simple, naïve questions that sophisticated people usually overlook. Try asking, "why," "why not," and "how" whenever you can.

Also ask awkward questions like, "Why is this a problem?" "Is that the real issue?" "Why have we always done it this way?" "What possibilities might exist that I haven't yet considered?" Aim to raise questions that haven't been asked before.

In your journal, write down a problem or a question that you're concerned with in your personal or professional life and ask: What? When? Who? How? Where? Why?

List a few small questions, maybe some that you've asked people over the last few days:

1. What were her symptoms

2. what do you think we need to do to improve communication

3. what is you perception of mid-level leadship

List a few big questions you've *wanted* to ask:

1. when are we going to slow down

2. what is the AF goal on

3.

Practice asking one or two big questions each day.

Serendipity

> Genuine beginnings begin with us, even when they are
> brought to our attention by external opportunities.
>
> —*William Bridges*

> Whatever you think you can do or believe you can do,
> begin it. Action has magic, grace, and power in it.
>
> —*Johann Wolfgang von Goethe*

There's a way to fill in your knowledge that takes into account curiosity, questioning, the learning process, and planning (but not too rigorously). It's called serendipity.

Serendipity could be defined as finding something better while in search of something else. Even though the popular definition of *serendipity* is "a happy accident," that doesn't adequately capture its potential. After all, it's not an accident. It's an attitude for action that comes from putting yourself in a frame of mind that will enable you to have a better experience than the one you originally planned. It's an attitude and an openness to take advantage of the unexpected, get ready for the unforeseen, and learn along the way. Surprises, well received, won't knock you off course. Instead, they'll reveal new directions. If you develop a capacity for it, you can learn more and do more than if you try to plan everything and are determined to stick to your plan.

If you stay focused on what you're pursuing and maintain good peripheral vision, you can be open enough to consider alternatives and find your right path.

I'm not talking about luck or coincidence. Luck implies that something just sort of happens to you without your control. Coincidence is clearly not a strategy; it just falls on you. With serendipity, you go about learning but with an attitude of watching for something better or more important than whatever you're already pursuing. With an attitude for serendipity, you're in active, passionate pursuit of something great; you're not sitting around waiting for something good to happen. You can even set objectives and pursue them until you discover something else. When you find a better way to fill the gap, you can abandon what you were previously pursuing, admit the new direction is better, and pursue that.

Although it may appear to some people that you're jumping from one activity to the next, you're consistently going after what you'd intended in the first place, even though you might not have realized it at the time. Serendipity is a means of getting where you really need to go.

When you maintain a high level of awareness and a willingness to listen to whole-body nudges, you can continue moving forward—but in accord with the new path you find yourself on. Think to yourself, "This might pull me in another direction, so I ought to keep myself flexible, spontaneous, and open to the unexpected feelings, and my senses."

You shift your urge from controlling every day to discovering your daily lessons as you go.

Filling Gaps As You Age

Aging, she discovered, was just another word for "growing"—and she was (finally!) at last growing into the person she always meant to be.

—*Jill Krasner*

If you fear that you're acquiring even more gaps in your knowledge as you grow older, it's worth noting that the memories of even elderly people work quite well, as long as they aren't pushed too hard. Experiments show that older people perform almost as well as younger people on memory and learning tests when given time and comfortable conditions. When they were put under stressful conditions, however, their performance dropped much more sharply than did the performance of their counterparts.

Over time, your knowledge of the world and your verbal ability improves, but the speed at which you store and recall new information slows. Older people perform most tasks, whether cutting with a knife, dialing a telephone, or remembering a list, more slowly than younger people do. You offset the loss of speed with fewer errors and wiser decisions.

As you age, you're also more able to organize information in useful and logical ways, which is necessary to find solutions to complex, real-world situations.

That's because not all types of memory are affected equally by age. Long-term memory—the memory you use to reference things—doesn't change nearly as much as does short-term memory, the kind you work with each moment.

Memories you hold in other parts of your body are likely to remain as easy to access as before, although they are now restrained by physical factors and a limited range of motion. In other words, you can still ride a bike, but do you want to?

7

Get Together

We're all in this together—by ourselves.

—Lily Tomlin

Weeds are flowers, too, once you get to know them.

—A. A. Milne

What do you do with other people that you don't do alone? You probably talk, laugh, strategize, argue, and do things you'd rather I not mention here. Much of who you are is a reflection of who you are with other people. Loner or group butterfly, we're social creatures who usually spend too little time understanding ourselves and our time together. I know who I am. You know who you are. But are you the same person you think you are with me as you are by yourself? And how does the difference influence what you learn? As you discover more about yourself, it's smart to also focus on learning from and with other people.

This chapter looks at how you work and learn with other people, how you identify and find others who can help you learn, how you gain knowledge you haven't gathered from your own direct experience, and how you can develop a learning community. By learning about learning together, you can get more from your relationships, as well as from your life as an individual, which will enhance everything you do.

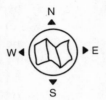

Road Map to This Chapter

Chapter 7 takes you to the following destinations:

▶ Learning your togetherness style

▶ Finding support from other people

▶ Creating a learning network

▶ Finding a learning community

▶ Working with a coach or a mentor

Togetherness Temperament

> By sharing and learning from common experience, people attain the high levels of rapport, empathy, trust and mutual understanding necessary to risk and embrace change together.
>
> —*Miriam Ricketts and Jim Willis*

When working on something, do you prefer to work alone or to work as a member of a group? Would you like only a few people to help, or does a large group make you feel more confident? People vary widely in how they prefer to learn with other people.

You might learn to be productive by yourself, choosing books over classes. Or you might decide that once you have thought things through, you can interact with other people, so you start with a book and then move on to a book group. Perhaps only after being introduced to a subject by another person or talking with someone else would you even consider trying to focus your attention when you're alone. Based on your togetherness style you may be consistent in how you approach others when you learn, or you may vary back and forth, depending on the type of work you're doing or the project you're trying to complete.

Consider Natasha, a college professor. As she and I walked around her campus, she recounted a class she had taught that required students to work together in small groups. Some of her students, brilliant mathematics scholars, were miserably failing the "working together" portion of their class, and she blamed her teaching skills. A brilliant mathematician herself, Natasha admitted that she loved working with one or two people at a time but didn't care as much for groups. She found it too distracting to try to understand many points of view. She was determined, however, to help these graduate students learn to *work together*—if not for their classmates, then for their future families and friends.

I hear this same issue come up repeatedly. Many people are uncomfortable learning in groups, but they want others to be able to do so.

Each of us has a style preference for how many people we appreciate being around at one time—be it for eating together, talking together, or learning together. Your togetherness number is frequently ignored when well-meaning people start creating groups in an effort to create "synergy" or collaboration. For some people, the size of the group that results is perfect. For others, the size of the group is counterproductive.

You can always stretch your comfort zone to work with more or fewer people, but without having a sense of your style, you might find yourself in uncomfortable situations and not understand why. I know many teachers, parents, and even business managers who feel that it's their obligation to make people work together, but I think that this should be tempered with a realistic attitude: Some people are just less comfortable learning with groups. Forcing people to work together doesn't help overcome that feeling.

To learn more and be more open with other people, it's helpful to look at a series of styles that influence how productive, happy, comfortable, and at ease—all of which directly influence learning—you are when working with other people.

What's Your Learning-Together Style?

Take a few minutes to complete the following questionnaire to assess how many people you prefer working with at a time. Begin by reading the words in the left-hand column. Of the three responses to the right, circle the one that best characterizes you. Count the number of circled items, and write your total at the bottom of each column.

1. I prefer to work . . .	✓Alone or in a pair.	With about three people. That seems to be the right number for me.	With as many people as possible.
2. Before I make a big decision, I tend to . . .	Research all I can or make a decision based on my own gut feeling.	✓Seek counsel from a few family members, close friends, or colleagues.	Talk with a wide variety of different types of people to find out how they might make their decision.
3. When coming up with new strategies, I'm likely to . . .	✓Discuss my initial thoughts with one other person.	Throw around some ideas with a small group (three people).	Brainstorm with a team.
4. When I'm by myself, I tend to . . .	✓Work on my own and appreciate the time.	Think about what a few other people might add to what I'm doing; I'm okay with the quiet time, but know it's temporary.	Go a little stir crazy, looking for ways to interact with other people.
5. When solving a problem, I tend to . . .	Figure it out for myself.	✓Bounce my ideas off a few other people before deciding how I'll proceed.	Consider as many perspectives as possible.
6. If I need to collaborate with other people, I . . .	Usually work on my own, then collaborate with one other person. I'm not fond of collaborating with other people.	✓Seek out two or three people who share a common perspective with me.	Love every minute of working with a big and diverse group.

(continued)

7. When I come upon something new or neat, I tend to . . .	✓Share it with one other person.	Send it to my close circle of colleagues or friends I know who will appreciate it.	Share it with as many people as possible.
8. When I don't understand something, I tend to . . .	Keep studying it, possibly asking one other person for insights.	Ask a few people for help.	✓Figure out who can offer a different perspective.
9. Most of the time I complete projects more effectively when I . . .	Have time alone.	✓Spend time with a few people I trust deeply.	Have many people to learn from, each contributing his or her unique perspective and talents.
10. I think that doing work with a group of people . . .	Wastes time.	✓Can work if it's a small group.	Is a great idea!
Total	**Alone/Pair** _4_	**Small Group** _5_	**Big Group** _1_

My togetherness style: _____Small Group_____

If you prefer to *learn alone* or with *one other person,* you find that the constant interaction that takes place in small groups and teams sometimes interferes with your ability to think and focus clearly.

If you prefer to work with a *small group,* you find that working with about three people enhances your ability to concentrate, and the constant interaction energizes you to the point that it helps you maintain focus.

If you prefer to be part of a *big* group, you know that team interaction energizes you, enhances your ability to concentrate and stay focused, and often sustains your interest in learning more.

Do You Learn Alone?

No man and no mind was ever emancipated merely by being left alone.

—John Dewey

If you prefer working by yourself, you might think, "Although I understand the value of teamwork, I'm more productive when I work by myself or with only one other person." When required to either listen to or work with several people, you may even become critical and anxious because you need extra time to focus and might need to sneak away to process materials alone or perhaps with one other person.

The constant interaction that takes place in small groups and teams sometimes interferes with your ability to think. You find that you're more productive when you first listen to other people and then take time alone to reflect and process the information.

When you begin a new project, you likely begin by working alone. This preference may lead other people to believe that you're not a team player. Even though you understand the value of teamwork, you simply find that you're more productive when you work by yourself for a time. Completing a portion of the project on your own works best for you because it gives you time to focus your attention and concentrate.

Your approach allows you, at your own pace and without all of the distractions, to plan how work should ideally progress. Once you've developed the basics, you're more prepared to work and learn with other people.

Tips for Solitude Learning

Here are some tips to help you learn from being alone or with one other person. If you think it would be useful to study something with another person, talk about your preference with someone with whom you seem to learn well.

> *Where to start.* Work with people you like, people who share similar interests, and those who have similar approaches. When this isn't possible, start by finding common ground.

> *Generate new ideas.* Brainstorm in a small group, and then work alone for a time.

> *Manage the situation.* Volunteer to complete tasks that you

can accomplish on your own (or with someone else), and then take your work back to the group.

Fake it. The most important class to take in order to improve your success in groups—acting lessons.

Make a little contact each day. Try to connect each day with one friend, a relative, or someone important to you and have a meaningful conversation. Rather than beginning with "Hi, how are you, what's new?" try "Tell me something wonderful you're doing for yourself." Social supports, even if they are from only one other person, help you feel better and cope easier with life.

Let other people know what you need. Sometimes, you will require other people's help to get your needs met. They can only help when they know what you need. When you ask for help from people, be specific.

If you must attend a party or a social gathering. . . . Find someone else standing alone and stand beside each other. Consider arriving late and leaving early.

Who Helps You Learn?

Name the people you spend time with who are lone learners or who probably prefer working with only one other person.

1. B

2. K

3. T

List some things you do that might bewilder these people and that you should probably avoid if you want to continue to learn with them.

1. Like you know their job

2. Talk on-on

3.

Do You Learn in Small Groups?

I'll pursue solitary pathways through the pale twilight meadow, with only this one dream: You come too.

—*Rainer Maria Rilke*

Does working with three people enhance your ability to concentrate and increase your productivity? If you're a small-group learner, constant interaction probably energizes you and helps you maintain your focus. When you have something to learn, you prefer small-team activities with two or three other people who are responsible, motivated, peer-oriented, and persistent. Some techniques that work well for you may include going around in a circle, each person offering his or her perspective and knowledge. You might also benefit from using case studies, creating scenarios together as a group, and role-playing.

Tips for Learning with Small Groups

These tips can help you learn with two or three other people. Spend time talking to people you enjoy learning with about their approach and what you can all do to get the most from your time together.

> *Generate new ideas.* Use the energy from the group to spark one another's thinking. Accommodate your preference by brainstorming your ideas with two or three people.

> *Divide the work.* Break full projects into smaller units and develop small groups to accomplish each task.

> *Manage the situation.* Volunteer for activities that are small–group based and where you can influence the types of activities you do together.

> *With groups.* When asked to speak in big groups, focus on two or three people right up front.

Who Helps You Learn?

Name several people you spend time with who also like learning in a small group.

1. C

2. K

3. S

List some things you might want to learn together.

1. Monitoring Styles

2. Lesson plans

3.

Do You Learn in Big Groups?

She was never a loner. . . . never made . . . to understand that life . . . in fact . . . is a solitary journey. . . . that the little Red Hen and the Engine That Could . . . did it themselves.

—Nikki Giovanni

Do you like working as a member of a team or with a big group? If you prefer to work with teams of at least four people or as large a group as can fit in a room, you probably prefer constant interaction, discussion, and working together. I suspect that team interaction energizes you, enhances your ability to concentrate and stay focused, and sustains your interest in whatever you do.

Tips for Learning in Big Groups

These tips will help you learn in big-group settings. Write some of your favorite tips on a big piece of paper, and post it somewhere in the room where everyone can see it.

Generate new ideas. Brainstorm ideas, options, and solutions with a team of people, the larger the better.

Prepare. Develop an agenda ahead of time to help keep everyone on track and on schedule so the group size never seems overwhelming.

Learn more. Develop a deeper understanding of group dynamics so that you can find ways for everyone to participate and feel like an important part of the team.

Think small. Remember that even big groups consist of individuals. Although large groups can provide a sense of anonymity, it's a mistake to ignore personal needs and interests.

Be responsible. If you have a habit of first seeking the help of many other people before trying something on your own, remember that you alone are responsible for seeing that your needs are met. Consider asking yourself for help first.

Create a crowd. Imagine a crowd when you need to work on your own. Cover a bulletin board with pictures of family, friends, or coworkers so you can feel as if they are right there with you when you are by yourself.

Who Helps You Learn?

What can you do to gather a large group of people together to learn? Throw a party? Sponsor a learn-in?

1. call meetings

2. team build Emails

3.

Name several people you know who also prefer learning in big groups. If you are unsure, ask them.

1.

2.

3.

Seek Support

> But for ourselves who know our plight too well, there is a
> need of great patterns to guide us, great lives . . . to inspire
> us, strong men and women to lift us up and give us
> confidence in the powers we, too, possess.
>
> *—Langston Hughes*

Even if you prefer learning with just one person, I encourage you to benefit from learning with the people around you and find support from those interested in helping.

How do you identify whom to learn with? No matter what your togetherness style, think about whom you can rely on to learn with.

Think over the following questions.

Among my family or friends, who has relevant experience with the situation I face or the topic I want to learn? *Jim, D, Bill*

Among people I work with, who is knowledgeable in the area I'm interested in learning more about? If it's not someone who works with me, whom do I know in the same field, yet from a different organization?

Doug

Who provides a good sounding board for ideas and plans that I want to explore? *K*

Whom do I trust to give me completely honest feedback?

Doug

Who removes obstacles and peels back distractions so that I can focus?

B

Who might remember what it was like to be a novice and can help me move from where I am to a more advanced skill level? (Novices and experts actually think about subjects in different ways, so someone who can't remember or appreciate an earlier stage may not be helpful in clearing up misconceptions or hidden assumptions.)

As I gain confidence in trying something myself, who will offer me insight and perspective to help me improve my outcomes?

Next, think about the types of information, advice, pushing, encouragement, and support you need to learn. Then think broadly about who could best help. Consider people outside your immediate family, circle of friends, and work group. Once you have a sense of who can help, contact them, explain why you need their help, and ask them if they're interested.

Sometimes people around you won't be able or willing to help. Does that mean you should quit? Sometimes, yes. Most of the time, *no!*

Your family, friends, and coworkers can be your biggest help or your greatest aggravation when you try to learn something new. You probably already know where your emotional support will come from, as well as which people in your life will resist. Here are some tips for talking with people around you to enlist their support.

> ***Share goals with your family.*** At home, talk about what you're learning with your children, your partner, your siblings, or your parents. Let them know why you're learning something and what they can do to help. Ask them to listen while you explain what you've learned, so that they can learn from it, too.

Share goals with your friends. You've probably acquired friends who share common interests, activities, or perspectives. If you let them know what you're learning, they will likely be able to offer you new information because their perspective is similar to yours but different enough to be useful.

Share goals with your coworkers. At work, solicit help from your manager, your peers, or other people in the organization who are knowledgeable about you or your interests. Let them know that you're committed to learning all you can.

This fill-in chart can help you determine what you need, identify people whom you can learn with, and figure out how to enlist their support.

What do I want to learn?	Who can help me learn it?	What approach should I take with them?
Mentoring	Boss	Need Help
Teaching	436+	
Classes		

As you build a support network, keep in mind that you need people to play different roles: sounding board, challenger, dialogue partner, role model, advisor, cheerleader, cohort, mentor, coach, and friend.

You increase your chances of learning when you don't try to do it alone. Identify people you can learn with and from—and enlist their help.

Create a Learning Network

> As we build relationships and tap into one another's
> networks, we create learning webs . . . fortified by different
> learners compounding their knowledge.
>
> —*Rich Persaud*

Another way to figure out who can help you learn is to write down the names of all the people you rely on for information gathering, problem solving, or learning in the moment. This is your learning network. These people can come from any area of your life. List at least ten names.

1. *whe*

2. *Dad*

3. *Doug*

4. *k*

5. *Tim K*

6. *Fsq*

7. *Relatives Ray*

8. *JA*

9. *Col D*

10. *Jim*

11. *Greg*

12. *CC*

Looking at those names, then think about which people fall into the categories and count how many are in each.

	Group
Family member (Do you rely on 7 family members to help you learn? If so, list that number in the column to the right.)	
Friend	3
Work together	4
Volunteer together	1
Neighbor	0

	Proximity
Same house/building	
Same neighborhood	
Same community	
Same city	
Same country	
Different country	

	Interaction
Never	
Sometimes	
Often	
Frequently	
Very frequently	

	Effort
1 hour or less per month	
2–3 hours per month	
1 hour per week	
2–3 hours per week	
1 hour or more per day	

	Time Known
Less than 1 year	
1–3 years	
3–5 years	
5–10 years	
10+ years	

	Hierarchy
Higher than yours	
Equal to yours	
Lower than yours	
Not applicable	

	Medium
Unplanned face-to-face meetings	
Planned face-to-face meetings	
Telephone	
E-mail	
Instant messaging	

	Gender
Same	
Different	

	Age
Younger by 6 years or more	
Your age, plus or minus 5 years	
Older by more than 6 years	

Now, look back on the list of names you made earlier, thinking about the composition of your learning network. What biases may affect how and what you learn? For example, do you reach out only to people near you or those who are already part of your routines, rather than to people who have more relevant information? Do you seek out people similar in age to you or people who look from a wide perspective?

Write in your journal what you might do differently in the future, who else you can approach, and what you've learned from this exercise.

Find a Learning Community

> Community is the missing piece in all of the self-help work I've seen. As a matter of fact, I'm sick of the term "self-help" because I really think it needs to be "community help."
>
> —*Cheryl Richardson*

One way to grow your network is to find and join a group of people whose members already come together, for a shared purpose, to do something that they couldn't do alone. Think about a PTA, a neighborhood association, or a special interest group (SIG), the AARP, or a diabetics support group. Each of those communities focuses on a topic that's important to its members and activities that they can do as a group.

You can find communities of people to help you learn by searching for such groups online; by reading flyers posted at your library, local bookstores, schools, and community centers; or by looking for groups listed in the newspaper.

If you get together regularly with other people, you will probably begin to build trust, which can help you to talk about your life, your feelings, your anxieties, and what you want to learn. In a community you can learn from other people's experiences and learn from different perspectives.

Find a Mentor

One way to find a community is through a mentor. A *mentor* is someone who is skilled or experienced in an area you're learning about, who uses their background to help you fill your learning gaps. You are responsible for sharing stories of success and failure, the resources and relationships you are using, and strategies you have tried. With this information, a good mentor can create appropriate events, engage you in provocative conversations, and generally share in your learning.

When seeking out a mentor, try to find someone who's encouraging, supportive, and a source of further suggestions. A mentor should be someone you feel comfortable with, who can also offer positive feedback, constructive criticism, and ideas to try.

Mentors can help you in the following ways:

- ▶ Show a genuine interest in your aspirations.
- ▶ Create challenging tasks and experiences.
- ▶ Appraise what you have learned but not criticize or blame you for mistakes.
- ▶ Let you solve problems and make your own decisions.
- ▶ Encourage your successes.

A mentor is especially useful in helping you to develop new skills and perhaps in preparing you for a new role, such as a job promotion or becoming a parent.

A mentor can choose activities for you that become progressively more challenging and can help you demonstrate your abilities.

Take, for example, Diane, a technical manager, who sat in on the meetings of a fellow manager and worked one-on-one with several team members, so that they could learn more about her group, the knowledge it had, and how the groups could help each other on future projects. She also saw that the two teams had complementary skills and, realizing that her team earned higher salaries and had more prestige, wanted to build a relationship in the event that the other team might join hers someday. Because of Diane's participation, team members learned from a manager whom they wouldn't normally spend time with, increased their technical competence, and found a job path they wouldn't have had access to otherwise.

Kevin, a recruiter, spent time with each of his staff members when they first hired their own employees. He explained what he looked for in a resume, listed the questions that he found had elicited the most telling answers, and demonstrated good listening skills, which helped them to be more aware of their new role and to experience the feeling of being hired by a truly terrific manager.

Julie, a birth doula, spends time with expectant parents before, during, and after their children's births. She complements the work of an obstetrician or a midwife by providing emotional support and nonpharmaceutical comfort measures. As the mother of three children and someone who has assisted in dozens of births, she helps parents through the process by increasing their confidence in and understanding of this incredible event.

If you're not interested in entering into a formal mentoring relationship, per se, you can still seek and offer mentor–like relationships with people around you. Think about people who have mentored you—formally or informally. How have they shared their expertise, experience, and knowledge and helped you find your way?

Show your appreciation by passing on the learning, wisdom, and caring you received to other people. Who can benefit from your attention and insights? You probably won't have to look far. Mentor one person and then another.

Find a Coach

From the sidelines in a sport, by your side at work, or in the front row of a presentation, giving hand signals to slow you down when you speak, coaches can help you work smarter because they see things you can't see from your own vantage point.

Coaching is different from mentoring, although the two are often confused. Mentoring relies on the mentor's expertise and resources to help you advance your learning, while coaching requires the coach's communication and intuition skills to help you see aspects of yourself and your aspirations.

A coach's role is to ask provocative questions, helping you to find insights into what is necessary to plan the next step. He or she provides this in different ways.

> *Through direct advice and information.* Drawing on their personal experience, as well as on their work with other people, a coach can provide a variety of experiences and resources to help you avoid the mistakes that others have made.

> *Through the focus and the structure of ongoing support.* To keep you on your learning path, a coach celebrates your successes, holds your hands through difficult times, and reminds you of promises you made to yourself when you have a hard time following through.

Through a mixture of means. A coach can monitor, encourage, and support your learning or can serve, ad hoc, at times when you just need another perspective.

At the beginning of your coaching relationship, establish and refine your direction, determine a schedule of how frequently you'll talk, and decide how you'll know when you've reached your destination. You can turn this into a formal process or can agree to approach this more casually.

If you are interested in working with a coach, these questions can help you strengthen your relationship so that you learn more from one another.

What do I want to be coached through?

Is this an appropriate topic for coaching?

What is the primary role I'm seeking (to be a sounding board for ideas and concepts, to ensure that I perform activities correctly, or to assess the limits of what I can do)?

How frequently will I be coached?

Which communication methods will we use to work together (will we use telephone, in-person meetings, e-mail, or a combination)?

What additional support do I require?

Find a Learning Partner to Read With

Another way to establish a learning relationship with someone is to collaborate in reading a book together. A *learning partner* provides you with a chance to share what you're reading.

▶ Choose a person you can trust.

▶ Be sure your learning partner has the time and the desire to complete the book.

▶ Read one chapter at a time before you meet.

▶ Pick a regular time, at least once a month, to talk in person or over the phone and review what you've read.

When you get together, use the following format to make your time together productive and supportive:

Start by sharing your success. What did you accomplish and learn since you saw each other last? How do you feel? Applaud each other for a job well done!

Review and reflect. Spend time talking through the chapter you've read for this meeting and complete any exercises from the chapter.

Take action. Decide on a specific action that you'll each take before you meet again.

Ask for help. Use the last quarter of your time to talk about what's stopping you from moving forward and then request any support you need.

Get unstuck. What's preventing you from learning more? What do you need to take action in spite of your fear? A helping hand? An extra telephone call to check in? A specific resource or referral?

You can use a similar approach with a partner for a new skill you each want to learn or a project you both need to complete. Identify a person (or a group) and organize a way to learn together over time.

8

Jump In

Deploy yourself. Strike hard. Try everything.

—*Warren Bennis*

God gives every bird its worm, but doesn't throw a worm into the nest.

—*Swedish proverb*

What would your family, your colleagues, and your friends think if they saw you do all the things you know how to do? What would you think of yourself? Many of us understand all sorts of things but never have the opportunity—or take the time—to try them out.

This chapter shows you that the more you experience, the more you learn. The more you learn, the more you know. The more you know, the more you can do. The more you learn about taking action, doing, and experiencing, the more you can accomplish on your own and with other people. Specifically, you'll learn how trying something actually helps you to learn faster and how playing with experiences helps you to create better experiences.

Life follows the situations we find ourselves in and happens in the context of these situations. For that reason, we need to be ready for opportunities that arise. By actually doing things, by allowing the unexpected to happen, and by getting comfortable in a wide variety of situations, we can learn almost anything and can improve almost every aspect of our lives.

Road Map to This Chapter

Chapter 8 takes you to the following destinations:

▶ Embracing experience

▶ Learning from doing

▶ Getting ready

▶ Getting going

▶ Keeping a learning log

Embrace Experience

What was the evidence I could write a poem? I just believed it. The most creative thing in us is to believe in a thing.

—*Robert Frost*

When we put our lives on hold in anticipation of a better time, we deny ourselves the opportunity to learn that even if a better time never comes, we will always have now.

—*Jeff De Cagna*

Think about how you've learned what has made you successful. If you're like most people, you've learned a great deal from your life experience—from talking about problems, working with different types of people, or even taking on responsibilities when you weren't prepared. Many of these challenges were not planned. They happened, you had to figure out what to do, and you learned from the doing.

In medieval times, educators thought that someday they would be able to teach people by drilling holes in their heads and, with a funnel, pouring information into their brains. Blech. Even though that seems funny now, we might still expect to learn new things through equally strange techniques. For example, many people believe they can learn to do something active by passively absorbing skills through their senses alone, without actually practicing or attempting the action. Although you take in information through your eyes and your ears, you ultimately learn by doing.

Doing, trying, and trying and doing again are at the core of the learning process. Remember how you learned to ride a bicycle? You took one action (maybe stepping on a pedal or balancing on the seat), saw the consequences of your action, and chose either to continue or to do something else. What allowed you to pick up the new skill was your active participation and the time you took to reflect on what you did. Doing taught you more than any lecture or book ever could. Experiencing it for yourself allowed you to do and encouraged you to do more.

In order to do something for the first time, you pull snippets of skills from your past experiences and you re-jigger them to do something new. The more variations you know from previous tries, the more options you have and the higher the likelihood that you'll find a method suited to your current situation. That agility can help you to react differently in similar situations and to develop creativity. Without a range of options, you have a narrow range of responses.

When you engage your senses and your body at a deep level, where you're more likely to remember what and how you've done something, you may be motivated to do it again because you know intrinsically that you can. This strengthens your pathways and also builds new ones. You learn what you're doing and can do it again.

You can use these methods to learn more by doing.

1. ***Get direct experience.*** For most of human history, people learned to survive by using a trial-and-error method of dealing with life's hurdles. Hunters learned by hunting, carpenters learned by building things. A few years ago, I worked with a group of Scandinavian business leaders. After we visited a high school in a rural part of the United States, one of the men in the group asked, "Why aren't these students learning?" He elaborated by asking, "Why are they at school, instead of learning a craft at home with their families?" In the community where he lives, most teens are farming or apprenticing to learn the skills they'll need to earn a living for the rest of their lives. Learning models vary widely around the world, and the one that most

U.S. schools have adopted is talk-based, instead of hands-on or based on direct experience. When you learn through direct experience, you gain confidence in yourself, get a tangible feel for the situation, and understand the subtle nuances that discussion rarely offers.

2. *Get out in the world.* Experience itself offers you so many more alternatives to try. In college, I co-led a water wilderness–learning program for students entering college. It was similar to programs offered by Outward Bound and the National Outdoor Leadership School (NOLS). During a month of portaging and camping under the stars in northern Ontario, twenty 17- and 18-year olds began to rely on themselves in new ways. Ben used his love for building relationships to figure out how he could work with as many different people as possible. Cara Lin used her nonlinear thinking to get us out of jams we didn't even know were up ahead. And Chris taught himself that he could thrive on an island by himself for three days, catching fish with his hands, cooking them on rocks in the sun, and teaching himself how to tell time from the shadows of trees.

3. *Try different roles.* Children play house, teacher, doctor, or astronaut because they crave doing. When you try on different roles and practice real-life skills in realistic ways, you learn the details of how to accomplish something which then builds pathways that can take you there. The Coro Foundation prepares people for community leadership and public affairs work by giving people a chance to immerse themselves in various roles. One of the organization's programs strings together a series of internships over a period of nine months. On a government internship, someone may land in the mayor's office, someone else in a planning department, and another person in public works. Together they learn how the city operates through the real-life roles they play.

4. *Take on a little at a time.* Start with a few small activities you can master and then apply them to similar activities. I once helped middle-school teachers who were getting a new computer for each classroom to overcome their nervousness that the students would be more expert than they were. On the Saturday after the computers arrived, still in boxes, a group of us met with the teachers in a classroom to work together assembling the equipment. We showed the teachers that computers are more resilient than teachers might have feared, and we cheered them on as they tried different things. That

night, they took their computers home, where they spent the next month getting familiar with them and using them for personal projects. After the month, they brought the computers back and integrated them into their classroom routines.

5. ***Get to the end at least once.*** Imagine moving to a new town and asking people for directions to the nearest grocery store. People determined to foster your learning skills rather than your grocery-acquisition skills might reply, "How do you *think* you get there?" That might force you to cycle through everything you know about the roadway system in your new town, but it wouldn't help you to get a quart of milk. If, on the other hand, someone said to go to the first stop sign, make a left, follow that road to the traffic light, turn left, then follow that road until you see the grocery on the left, you'd be there in a few minutes. On the way home, because you felt so good about your success, you might take a different route back and the next time, yet another way. Doing helped to cement what you learned through those simple directions and gave you the leeway that helped you branch out.

6. ***Get out of your comfort zone.*** When I first begin to work with a new group of adults, I pass around a basket of toys for participants to fidget with. I also suggest that during our time together they stand, walk around, and move, whenever they feel like it. A few years ago, I facilitated a program for grade-school librarians and attempted the same approach. At first, they didn't want to take the toys, and then they didn't want to stand up. Gradually, a few of them tried what I suggested. At that point, the entire dynamics of the room changed, and the librarians became remarkably receptive to the idea. They made the connection that for some people, being still could prevent learning. When they physically did what I had suggested all along, they understood.

7. ***Get only basic instructions.*** When you receive basic instructions, you can use them to catapult yourself into taking the next step on your own. As you work along, pay attention to errors and try out various ways to recover from them. Stop for a few moments whenever you finish a step, to think about what you did and how you did it before trying the next step. At some point, after you figure out several ways to proceed, scramble the sequence to see if you can do things in a different order. This is how I learned to use a word

processor for the first time. I began to explore the computer, looked around at the menus, and began to understand—for myself, in my own language—what this new tool offered me. Soon enough, I was hooked. I learned to use that word processor in far less time than it would have taken to read the manual, and I was able to get started much faster that way.

8. *Give it a go.* Sometimes, the only way you will find out that you can do something is just to do it. The Irish poet David Whyte tells a story of his time as a marine biologist, knowing in his heart he should be a poet. A friend visited David, and they got to talking about his desire to be a poet. The friend suggested that each day David do one thing as a writer. He suggested that David write a poem, write a letter mentioning that he wrote a poem the day before, research the poetry market, read something on poetry, and do this for a year. At the end of the year, "You will be a poet," his friend said. And David was. Now, he is one of my favorite poets and maybe one of yours.

9. *Do it now.* My dad used to drink his coffee from a mug that read, *Do It Now*, implying, "Why wait?" My brother's death, which I faced at such a young age, calibrated my sense of what constitutes *now* and filled me with a lifelong dedication to live a full life—in a way that accounted for what made me special and that helped me to use my gifts. The notion of going ahead to do something as soon as possible—and learning from it along the way—remains with me each day.

10. *Be a doer.* For you nondoers—those who have read the exercises in this book but skipped doing them—recognize that you aren't challenging or growing your pathways. You aren't amending, lengthening, challenging, and revising them, either. With this approach, you will move forward gradually, but your previous pathways will always limit your potential. I once had a boss who wasn't much of a doer. He was great at asking people to remove obstacles in my path, but unless he had an action-oriented employee who took on some of his work, he was bound to fall behind. For most of us, at least some of our work entails getting up from our desks and actually doing something (and that means more than just walking around). "He's not much of a doer" implies that he hasn't gotten much done, and he's probably not really learning much.

Keep a Doing Log

> Only those who will risk going too far can possibly find out
> how far one can go.
>
> —*T. S. Eliot*

One way to see what you've done is to keep a written record of your experiences, what you've learned from them, and what to do differently next time. You can keep your *Doing Log* right beside other notes in your journal or in a separate place. In your log, record your observations and conclusions, as well as how to do something better or differently if you do it again.

After years of writing down what I've done, I find that the three most helpful things to capture are these:

1. What was the experience?

2. How did I do it?

3. What variations might I try next time?

Here is a basic sample.

Experience	How did I do it?	Variations
Got out of bed	Rolled over and put my feet on the ground.	Maybe try a stretch before actually standing up?

The format you choose isn't as important as eliciting these three pieces of information.

How frequently you write down what you do is up to you. It might be once a day or once per week, but try writing at least today and for the next few days as you finish this book. Try not to reserve the log for only your most striking or dramatic experiences. If you do, you might miss everyday happenings and incidents, which also build those pathways to learning and doing more.

I can almost hear you say, "Write down *everything?* You must be joking!" If you write for even three days you will likely begin to see important patterns such as why you're tired at the end of each day, why you ought to give yourself more credit for what you do, and that by building some reflecting time into your day you'll be able to turn routine tasks into useful lessons that are worth learning about.

If you have an aversion to writing things down, talk into a tape recorder and have it typed out later. Writing or talking about an experience, and what you learn from it, can help you transform it from a memory into a useful resource.

Once you've mastered the basic Doing Log, you may see other applications or variations on the theme. For instance, I keep a log in the back of a cookbook that I've created with my favorite recipes. I've written things like, "This zucchini bread has a better consistency if you grate the zucchini by hand, rather than putting it in a food processor." Because I aim to keep meal preparation to under twenty minutes, I keep track of what I did and what I should do differently next time to speed up my work even more.

Get Ready

> I find myself watching and listening for the moments when the right word or gesture changes everything: those moments when talented people play with a possibility, or experiment with a new idea, and *they get it.* The energy and excitement in the group shifts to another level. It's a high. It's fun to watch.
>
> —*Michael Schrage*

> It's all about readiness: being ready to do something, not just learning about doing.
>
> —*David Grebow*

There is a big difference between doing something in order to be prepared and taking action to create neural pathways, and begin the process of improving it, doing it again, or learning from the experience. The best reasons for jumping in, trying something, and doing it now are to ready yourself and to improve your reaction time—how quickly you recover from surprise. It's unrealistic to expect yourself to be thoroughly prepared for every situation anyway. Find your balance between disciplined inquiry (What else do I need to know?) and playful discovery (What do I find out when I just play around with these ideas?).

Take, for example, Earl, a performance strategist, who wanted to learn to play golf. He read a book about the history and the etiquette of golf, watched a videotape of great golfing moments, and even bought a computer golf game. Then he attended a golf seminar at a local driving range, found a pro who gave him lessons, learned to simulate the swing, practiced putting, and sliced and diced balls at the driving range all weekend. From his first tee shot on his first hole, he spent hours swinging all the clubs, in every type of weather and condition, failing and succeeding, practicing and practicing even more, before he was ready to play golf. He was ready when he could then perform these actions under various circumstances. At that point, he may not have been ready to win the game, but at least he was ready to play.

The difference between doing something for the heck of it and doing it in order to be ready to do it again is in learning to adjust. Adapt and adopt, develop a sense of timing, find meaning for yourself, get an accurate perception, and gain a sense of confidence that whatever you set your sights on isn't that hard after all.

These practical tips will help you get ready to learn, to try, and to do whatever you want to do.

1. ***Practice.*** Do you take time to fail and succeed, to adopt and adapt, and get ready? Or, do you expect to just be prepared by watching and thinking, even though you don't take time for actually doing? Chinese culture values practice so highly that the expression for learning is made up of two symbols—one represents studying and the other, practicing constantly. When you practice, you play with possibilities, you experiment with new ways of working, and you can understand things you couldn't understand through any other means. Learning comes from activity, not from reaching the goal. Along the way, practice builds and strengthens the breadth of your pathways, which then help you go further and do more. It takes approximately six hours after you practice for the memory of a new physical skill to be stored permanently.

I realized this when the women in my neighborhood convinced me I wanted to learn to play tennis. I had held a tennis racket, I had played racquetball before, and I was married to a skilled tennis player, so I thought it would be easy to learn to play. It wasn't. I could intellectually grasp what to do, but that didn't mean I was ready to play. When you live with people who love tennis, you watch tennis on TV, you watch them play, and you listen to conversations about tennis. It seemed so simple. What I wasn't so good at was practice. When I did however, my game turned around. It wasn't so much what I learned in tennis practice, but the fact that I was moving. I learned from my mistakes, I learned with parts of my body that weren't in my head, and I could begin to feel when I was doing everything right.

2. ***Try it as if you mean it.*** Are you halfhearted when you practice a new skill? Do you use second-rate tools, practice at a time when you'd never really try something for real, or go about your practice time in a frenzy? When you practice in order to get yourself ready, create similar conditions to those you're aiming to face, but add each factor in slowly, so that you can adjust each step of the way.

   One of my favorite examples is of Dean, an entrepreneur, who taught his daughter to ride her bicycle in under an hour. He explained his technique of three stages. First, he put on training wheels so that she got an idea of how a bicycle maneuvers. Next, he removed the training wheels *and* the bicycle pedals. This enabled her to focus on using her feet to push off for balance, when necessary. As a result, she experienced the genuine feeling of balancing and moving forward. She naturally gained the rhythm and the sensation without being distracted by figuring out what to do with her feet. When he put the pedals back on, it was only one small addition. She continued to use her feet to push off and stop. Not much had changed, but now she could ride.

3. ***Put in the time.*** Do you take enough time to let your muscles and your pathways adjust, or do you rush through the most basic activities, thinking that your understanding of them is enough for you to move on? When you put in the time, you physiologically make connections between your body and your brain to execute a specific movement and, in turn, what you aim to do. You respond from a collection of previous played-with possibilities, and you experiment with new ways of moving. Ongoing practice, over time, expands your

snippets of collected experiences, which you can pull together to adapt to new situations, and which ultimately are there to help you try something new.

Pick up a baseball and a bat, practice your swing long enough, and you'll eventually learn how to hit the ball. The *New York Times* music critic Harold Schonberg wrote of a European conductor who wasn't really very skilled but who performed fabulous music because he kept his orchestra in rehearsal for each concert for a full year. Most of us can acquire at least some proficiency at almost anything, if we just put enough time into it.

4. *Make a leap.* Are you willing to venture a guess at the answer, at how to do something, at where to begin, and then make the jump? Sometimes, in order to learn new things, you need to make a leap of faith that you'll be okay and that you'll learn so much along the way that you might as well get started. You say to yourself, "Sure, I'll try. What's the worst thing that could happen?"

Floyd, a former colleague whom I gave talks with, could teach anyone anything, as long as someone in the room knew the answer. He would look at the questioner and, with a sly grin, turn the question back to the group, "Excellent question. What do you all think?" Inevitably, someone who knew the answer would be eager to reply. Floyd's ability to take a leap taught him quite a bit about subjects that other people thought he already knew.

5. *Act cool.* Are you able to pretend that you're enthusiastic for long enough to actually become enthusiastic, be calm enough to become calm (or find an appropriate place to blow your top), or look interested long enough to hear something interesting from someone else? Sometimes a little acting skill can help you get ready by enabling you to act as if you *are* ready until you find the courage to do what's next. This works because there's a relationship between your expressions and your emotion. What your face and body show, your cellular emotions will match.

At a meeting for recent college graduates who were looking for advice on how to succeed in business today, panelists were asked about the best things we had done when we were young that prepared us for our careers. People to the right and the left of me said that they'd found mentors or coaches. Other people took communications courses in graduate school. One had a job as a journalist, which helped him to focus on the facts and be able to write quickly. I said that the acting skills I picked up from theater productions I'd been in during high school had proved very valuable. Although I wouldn't suggest that anyone act instead of being authentic at work, there have been moments when I pretended to keep my cool while everyone around me wilted. Because of this, I received more interesting (and sometimes more challenging) projects than my coworkers did. Other times, I could appear calm, even when my heart was pounding ferociously, long enough to learn more and actually make a good decision or to alleviate the tension in the room.

6. *Immerse yourself.* Do you try to watch from the sidelines, or do you join in the action? By getting into the middle of a situation, you can feel the emotions around you, pick up the pheromones of other people involved, and generally get a better sense of a situation than you could by observing from a distance. Although actually throwing a baby into a swimming pool would be considered irresponsible, the "sink or swim" metaphor contains some truth.

   I lived in Kenya for part of a year in college. Although I took a few basic language courses before I left, when I lived with a family that spoke no English, I picked up their language much more easily than I could have through any class because I was immersed in their environment, I heard the Swahili everywhere I went, and I needed to find the correct words (or, at least, the accompanying hand gestures) to convey my meaning about everything from food portions to sleeping arrangements to washing my clothes. I also learned how to cook meals in the style of the family I lived with, because the family women had the task of preparing large feasts for marriage ceremonies in the local community. I had never prepared food for four hundred people, but when given a large bowl, mounds of ingredients, and some basic instructions, I quickly learned out of necessity, and I seemed to soak up everything I needed to know.

7. *Imagine.* Do you imagine how you will approach something, walk through every step of the process, and visualize not only what you're trying to do but how you'll do it? When you visualize successfully doing something in your mind's eye, you establish the pathways and the connections that would be stimulated by the real-life experience, and you trigger the same whole-body circuitry. Mental rehearsing fixes the various pathways and routes of association in your thoughts.

When you then take action in the real world, you have the sense that you have done this before, and you can do it again. Every time you pull up that image, you strengthen the route to it, in the same way that a path in the woods becomes clearer and more defined each time you walk it.

Charles Garfield, who worked for years with the astronauts at NASA, watched them rehearse everything in simulators. Later he made a study of peak performers, people who were experts in what they did. It struck him that they also used simulations, but their form of simulation was mental—they all used imagery to help them succeed.

8. *Play.* Do you feel as anxious when you're just playing around as when you think you're doing something for real? Play allows you to learn quickly from your mistakes, without suffering serious consequences. Play is life's natural learning curriculum. It provokes you to constantly improvise and invent new responses, and play's random surprises keep you interested. When you play, you're motivated to repeat skills you just learned, without having any sense of working toward a goal. That helps you to build both the breadth and the strength of your pathways and to understand new things. Also, if you see someone's performance getting a great response, it may encourage you to try it yourself. Playing provides you with vital but nonthreatening feedback, so that you can learn from your mistakes, adjust your approach, and try again so that you can improve your technique.

When wild cats play, they're acquiring hunting skills and learning to escape predators. From playing house to playing teacher and police, children play and learn to make a life. The games that children play are a means to explore, with no ends in mind, no goals, no limitations. Play provides a means for learning in an environment of low threat, high feedback, and limitless fun, where many chances to learn are inherent in the activity.

9. *Give yourself some leeway.* Do you expect to master something the first time you do it? Most activities don't work that way. If you think that nothing should be tough, that you should know how to do everything, and do it well the first time, be persistent, but also patient. We learn from our mistakes and from adapting our behavior the next time we try.

Children adapt their behavior intuitively when they learn to walk. First they roll over. Then they sit up; next, pull up. They try to balance, using their arms, feet, and body. Once they master balance, they let go, then take one step, and fall. Because they don't like the feeling of falling, they try to step again. After two steps, they try three. Soon they can run. They have no preconceived notions that they should be great runners right from the beginning, and neither should you.

10. ***Embrace ambiguity.*** Are you convinced that once you can do something, it will always work out a certain way? There is rarely just one way to do anything, and the sooner you can embrace the multiple methods, the various degrees, and drop any illusion of certainty, the easier you can allow ambiguity to become part of your regular routines. Instead of working toward one right way, consider elements of right ways.

When your first reaction to a question is, "Gee, I don't know," try asking yourself, "Well, if I did know, what might I say?" If you proudly think to yourself, "I've got THE answer," consider asking, "Might there be another right answer?" And when there seems to be nothing but vagueness around you, ask, "What are the elements of this ambiguity that I can learn from along the way?"

9

Pace Yourself

Live as if you were to die tomorrow; learn as if you were to live forever.

—*Mohandas Karamchand Gandhi*

You rush a miracle, you get a rotten miracle.

—The Princess Bride

Even when you have the best intentions to learn more, you might be sabotaging yourself by the pace you set for yourself. It might be too fast, it might be too slow, or it might not be accommodating enough when situations change. Different types and stages of learning warrant special speeds.

This chapter introduces you to the role that rate, reflection, and rumination play in what and how much you learn. Then you can adjust and improve your pace in order to move at a tempo that's optimal for what you're learning. When you discover how your rhythm influences learning, you're more able to choose the appropriate approach.

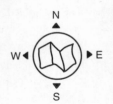

Road Map to This Chapter

Chapter 9 takes you to the following destinations:

▶ The three learning speeds

▶ Working faster than thought

▶ Timing your learning right

▶ Engaging your peak learning time

▶ Scheduling

Take Your Time

As an energetic youngster, I wanted everything faster. Then one day my grandmother asked me if I could speed up the weather or make my hair grow faster. With these questions, she helped me see that you shouldn't try to rush some things. Everything works on its own schedule.

Thoughts, too, work at different speeds. You work through some ideas seemingly faster than thought. Other concepts take seconds, minutes, hours, days, or even years to grasp. You can speed up the time it takes to make sense of some things by learning new techniques and gaining more knowledge, but you can't just make up your mind to think fast.

Here's an overview of the three predominant thinking speeds. By understanding them, you can begin to identify the appropriate one for your situation and for what you're trying to learn.

Faster Than Thought

> I hate everything that merely instructs me without
> increasing or directly quickening my activity.
>
> —*Johann Wolfgang von Goethe*

Some situations demand an instantaneous response. The fastest thoughts you have are so fast, you don't know you're having them. They seem *faster than thought.* Sometimes your brain isn't involved in the reaction or you've practiced so much that your muscles just know how to respond.

How does this work? When you first learn a physical skill, you need to pay close attention, mentally and physically. But as you become savvy responsibility shifts from connections all over your brain to connections in lower parts of your brain, and you rely more on the memory in your body. This frees up parts of your brain to attend to something else.

Mental skills (such as learning that 4 × 4 = 16) also move down from higher parts of your brain to lower parts of your brain and into your body as they become *automatic.*

Initially, when you drove a car, it was a challenge to learn how to stay between the lines while also shifting, braking, looking both ways, quickly glancing in the mirror, and occasionally using the turn signal. Over time, you do all of these things faster than thought, without paying attention to them, and that makes you a safer driver.

Inevitably, this also has its downside. When you acquire a skill to the point that it's automatic, you may learn less and find it difficult to adapt. You may no longer notice a change in circumstances, and, for instance, find yourself driving through a newly placed stop sign at a familiar intersection that had no sign before.

Reflecting

My body has certainly wandered a good deal, but I have an uneasy suspicion that my mind has not wandered enough.

—*Noel Coward*

Many men go fishing all of their lives without knowing that it is not fish they are after.

—*Henry David Thoreau*

The second pace is *deliberate,* reflective, comparative thinking, which works best when you face a situation you can describe or you face a problem to solve. It's slower than "faster than thought" but not quite the slow ruminating addressed a little later. It's the middle speed and helps you understand more than the other two speeds do. This thinking speed is better for finding answers and solutions than for examining open-ended questions.

This pace is appropriate, for example, when you want to learn where your family wants to go for dinner. You will want to consider how many people are going? How much can you afford? What kinds of food does everyone enjoy? How long is it before mealtime? This doesn't happen in an instant and doesn't improve if you take a long time. The trouble is that many people tend to treat all situations as if they were solvable problems.

Reflect on Experiences

You deliberate most when you're at the reflecting stage in the learning process, when you connect how you learn with some previous experience and you consider how this might offer you a new way to act. Using the previous example, what you learn from your family members about their food choices will help you determine which restaurant to choose.

When you reflect, you can also look at what other people say, what other people have done, and how what you're learning fits with what you know. You might even make a few predictions and think about how what you're learning could change your situation.

Reflection also helps you to clarify how well you're doing, how much you've learned, and where you might need to make changes.

As you reflect, use these questions to help focus your thoughts.

How did the experience I just had help me?

What are my reactions to this experience? What do I think about it? What do I feel?

What do I wish I had done differently?

What can I learn from my reactions?

Take time to reflect as often as possible. At the very minimum, when you want to learn something new, reflect on it once each week for ten minutes. After you establish a pattern, it may be easier to increase the frequency and the duration of your reflection time.

Spend part of your drive home asking yourself, "How will I use what I learned today?" or "What are the implications of what I learned on the people I work with or on my community?" If you do, you'll find yourself remembering more of your experiences and can discover innovative applications for what you've learned that you can use next time. Reflecting might also improve your drive time if you consider, "Last time I went that way, I found a detour. I shouldn't go that way again for another few weeks."

Keeping a journal is another useful way to reflect. As you write, you might become aware of thoughts you didn't notice before. You can use your journal to consider the previously listed questions. Just start writing.

Reflect on Mistakes

Everyone makes mistakes. You can learn from them if you reflect on your errors and determine how to adjust your approach so that you can do something different next time.

Ask yourself, "What did I learn from the last thing I messed up?" Most people remember everything they ever flubbed but almost nothing about what they then learned. If you didn't learn anything, then it wasn't a mistake but rather a waste of your time! Nothing works as well as a mistake to focus your attention and invite you to learn more.

Rather than viewing mistakes as frustrating roadblocks, regard them as guideposts, indicating what you still ought to learn.

Next time, try to respond this way:

1. Admit that you made the mistake.

2. Look for the lesson that is embedded in the mistake.

3. Devise a plan so that you won't make the same mistake again.

4. Celebrate what you've learned about yourself.

I remind myself of a few statistics when I reflect on mistakes. Thomas Edison was so focused on doing, learning, and reflecting along the way, he gave himself and his assistants *idea quotas.* To reach those quotas, they couldn't be afraid to make mistakes or to produce something mediocre in order to arrive at something outstanding. In order to acquire his 1,093 patents, he made more than 100 times that many mistakes. A study of 2,036 scientists throughout history found that the most respected scientists produced not only great works but also many bad ones.

Because my family prized learning and taking chances above almost anything else, I was fortunate to realize early on that mistakes were opportunities to learn from. My dad, a one-time history teacher in the Chicago city schools, wasn't talkative (similar to many fathers of his era), but when I made a mistake, especially mistakes involving him, he'd inevitably ask one key question, "What did you learn?" His approach gave me a chance to learn instead of berate myself.

At the WD-40 Company, the people who make the oil in the blue and yellow can talk about what they've learned every chance they get. At a meeting of global brand managers, for example, everyone presented five or six hard lessons he or she had learned in the last year. People used to hide their mistakes, but they've found that when they share their *learning moments*—even the times when they screwed up and learned something as a result—they become cheerleaders for one another, and it helps them not to make the same mistake.

You can turn mistakes into your own learning moments by asking the following questions. Reflect on one from the past year and examine what you can now learn from it.

1. What caused this?

2. What worked inside the overall mistake?

3. What can I learn from what happened?

4. Who can help me do something different next time?

5. Where do I go next?

Make a commitment to learn something from every mistake or thorny experience you face. Lessons are there for the learning; however, the mistake itself won't reach out to teach you. Reflect on mistakes and move on.

Reflect on Yourself

It takes courage to reflect on your experiences and your mistakes. If it's too painful to try, work up to it by thinking of the last truly *odd* thing you did.

Try reflecting on the experiences with the following questions. You might also want to write these questions in the back of your journal or post them nearby so that you can look at them each day.

What went well?

What didn't go well?

What *could* I do differently next time?

What *should* I do differently next time?

What observations struck me the most?

What images, stories, or metaphors capture the essence of the situation?

What did I notice about myself?

What's the most important lesson for me to take away from this?

What potential new opportunities have come as a result?

What questions do I still have?

Review

Here is a quick technique to help you learn from what you reflect on and remember what you learn. This method works with almost anything, although my example is for written information.

While information is fresh in your thoughts, take one minute to review it. Note key words or ideas at the center of what you want to retain. Identify patterns and organize the material in the way that seems best for you.

Scan the material again, to notice any additional information you may have missed.

Then review on a regular schedule. Take thirty seconds or so to reflect on the patterns you've identified after a day, a week, a month, six months . . . and you'll remember it for life.

This method also works when you listen to a recording, watch a video, or make notes for yourself.

Ruminate

> You cannot teach a man anything; you can only help him
> discover it within himself.
>
> *—Galileo*

Have you ever deliberated over a seemingly unsolvable problem that made you tired and wore you out? Eventually, you probably gave up and decided to sleep on it. The next morning, while brushing your teeth, you may have returned to the dilemma with a fresh insight into the obvious next step to take.

Beneath reflection is a more playful, less clear-cut, leisurely level of learning—*unhurried*. That's where you ruminate and mull things over;

where you let new information settle into your whole body. That's where you give what you're thinking, and thinking about doing, a generous time to rest.

Ruminating happens when you let what you learn stir around in your subconscious—not directly thinking about it but, rather, just letting it be. This is where you incubate new ideas and where you bring together things you've learned that haven't come together earlier. Maybe you have a conversation with someone and recognize a link with something you were thinking about earlier today. Maybe you see a pattern that hasn't occurred to you before.

This third speed of thinking is associated with creativity and wisdom. Even though you can't train for it, teach it, or engineer rumination, you can cultivate it.

Think slowly when you're not sure which factors to consider or what questions to ask or when an issue is too subtle to be captured by familiar categories. If the problem isn't "Italian or Indian food for dinner?" but how best to manage a difficult situation at work, or whether to completely give up your job to go into the forestry service or start a family, you might be better advised to quietly ponder, rather than to search frantically for an answer.

In rumination, your subconscious sorts through all the information you've collected, all the possibilities you've played with, puts everything together, and finds an order that will help you make sense of your situation.

Sadly, our culture usually ignores and undervalues these unhurried ways of learning, treating them as insignificant or frivolous. Western society seems to have adopted as its default mode only one speed—deliberate. To try this slow thinking, you need to relax and feel comfortable accepting whatever shows up.

A strategy professor from Harvard University once said something to a group of us at a conference that supports this notion. She said that the most important part of her job is putting her feet up on her desk to think and reflect, yet that's inevitably when her colleagues walk by and assume that she's not working anymore. However, she explained, this was actually when she did her real work.

It's an age-old problem. When Leonardo da Vinci was painting *The Last Supper*, he worked intensively for days, then he'd leave. The church prior at Santa Maria della Grazie said something to the Duke of Milan, who had originally arranged the contract. "Where is Leonardo? Get him back on the scaffolding to complete this work." Leonardo wouldn't hear of it and said, "Men of genius sometimes accomplish more when they work less." He explained that he needed time to integrate his thoughts and that sometimes the most productive work happened when he wasn't on the scaffold but, rather, walking through Milan.

Ruminating is a stage of learning at the slowest pace (for a fixed period of time), but that can help you find those fleeting brilliant moments when all of a sudden, in a flash, you make a connection or recognize something that you hadn't noticed before.

Before I figured this out, I was awful at this stage, always on the go. Then I realized that some of the fastest learning I've ever done has taken me the longest period of time to find. I had this "Aha!" experience when my division leader at Microsoft asked a group of us, "What did you learn in the shower this morning?" She wasn't prying into personal details with the kind of invasiveness Microsoft has sometimes been known for; it was her way of asking, "What happened when you stopped thinking intentionally about work, let the water pass over your head, and allowed your best ideas to bubble up?"

I frequently ask a slightly different question of people. I ask, where do you do your best thinking? For me, the answers come when I walk our dog in the woods, while on vacation, or even when leisurely walking through the grocery store.

Great learning occurs when the incubatory power of slow thinking is combined with the flash from fast thinking. I find it helpful to focus intensely and then let go completely, so that the rumination period and my imagination can take over. At that time, I need to listen to the subtle, quiet voice of whole-body intuition before I begin my next intensive period of hard work.

When you ruminate, you access a deeper level of learning that you simply can't rush. This learning method, although it's rarely talked about in school, has been used throughout history. Albert Einstein played the violin when he wanted to make connections. Winston Churchill painted landscapes to see things from another angle.

When you learn something new, your thoughts may be patchy, they may not yet make sense, and you may not know where to focus. When you give those thoughts a rest, you let other senses, your gut feeling, your sense of wonder, your questioning—those slow ways of knowing—boost what you can learn by giving them a chance to self-organize.

If you think you're too busy to think slowly, consider Brenda, a leadership strategist and one of the busiest people I know. As she began to write her doctoral dissertation, amid four other projects, her daughter became ill. Brenda cleaned out her home office, fearing that she wouldn't be able to return to it for a long time. She taped her notes around the room and then closed the door. Occasionally, she took a break from caring for her daughter and walked around the office, reflecting on the yellow pages covering the walls. After several long weeks, her daughter regained strength. When Brenda sat down at the computer again, she found new patterns in her work and immediately realized which material was extraneous. It took her just two weeks to complete all of her writing. No amount of intentional deliberation could have produced better results.

Where do you have your best ideas? When do you push and when do you let patterns emerge? Spend a little time each day letting what you learn be with you, and then reflect a little on how it connects.

Slow Down

> There cannot be a crisis next week. My schedule is already full.
>
> *—Henry Kissinger*

Sometimes, I wonder if the difficulty we face learning to work at different speeds is from listening to our heads and our voices, instead of listening to our whole selves. If you work hard all the time, you might override the subtle messages of the intuition.

To tap into the easygoing ways of learning, dare to wait. Find the courage to look at those areas your internal observer has ignored for a long time.

These tips will help you cultivate unhurried thinking:

1. ***Sleep on it.*** When I face a challenge I can't seem to get through, or I'm trying to understand something that's just not coming together, I write it down in my journal before going to bed at night, to get clear on the crux of the issue. Then I forget about it and go to sleep. Immediately in the morning when I wake up, while I'm still in that semi-sleep state, I start writing the first thing that comes to me in my journal. Sometimes I give it a jump-start by saying, "So the solution to this problem

is . . ." or, "How this fits together is . . ." And insights start pouring out. I find that I can use this method for all sorts of different situations in my work life, my family life, and my relationships.

2. *Vary your pace.* Although your coworkers or your family may not appreciate that sometimes you accomplish more when you work less, find ways to vary your pace between intense work and unhurried thinking. I'm not suggesting that you just sit back and only be intuitive or lie around all day. If you do, you won't have anything to incubate. Rather, find a rhythm between intense focus and reflection, then let go, shifting modes into a more unhurried and receptive pace. After you've taken in a lot of information, go for a walk, put your head on the table, or do some of the stretches described earlier in this book.

3. *Do nothing every once in a while.* The problem with learning by doing is that some of us do it *too* well. You might be one of those people who carry files and reading material everywhere you go, to review in restaurants, at the 2-minute traffic light in the middle of town, and even during kids' carpooling. For me, this might be hereditary. On a recent visit from my mom, we spent a day visiting friends and relatives, going shopping, and walking around the downtown area. When we got back, she uttered, "I don't know why I'm so tired. I haven't done anything all day." If this sounds like your family, too, I encourage you to do nothing once in a while, so that you can learn from what you've done. I urge you to add to your to-do list entries that say "rest," "relax," "ruminate," and "think slow."

4. *Support other people in doing less.* Two of my most overachieving friends and I (affectionately called the "Full of It Club" because we are *full of* life, love, to-do lists, and plenty of opinions), started an online support group, sharing stories of times when we do less and slow down. It takes time to write up what we didn't do, but the encouragement and the inspiration have helped us in untold ways. One posting began with this note, "On Memorial Day, I spent six glorious hours in my garden, sometimes thinking about nothing, sometimes daydreaming, sometimes praying, and sometimes staring at the mountains. And there are nights when I wait until everyone is in bed, lights out, and sit and admire the view of the city below, with no intellectual agenda. And I'm hoping not to wait months for the next time." Think about doing

something similar with your friends. There is nothing like doing less in the company of other people.

5. ***Get some sleep.*** If you feel exhausted and overwhelmed, you'll find it hard to relax, reflect, or ruminate because your precious energy will be spent on just surviving. A good night's sleep is no longer a luxury; it's a necessity. Your body and your brain need more than just relaxation-style downtime to replenish and rejuvenate your energy. You need deep sleep. At least once a month, sleep longer than you feel you have a right to, take an afternoon nap, or ask someone to watch your children so that you can catch up on missed sleep. If you feel as though you've been running on fumes for a while, you probably are. Make deep rest a priority.

I have a challenge for you. For the next week, take time every day to be alone with your thoughts. Hide your to-do list. Turn off the radio in your car. Look at the clouds. Go to bed a half-hour earlier. Do something because, well, just because. And get as much sleep as you possibly can. Then, when you've figured out how to be idle—how to do or think or talk about anything that pleases you, even for a brief amount of time every day, visit my web site and let me know how it goes.

Thinking slowly or reflecting on what you've done isn't a result of having nothing to do. It's a function of your perspective. Idle time isn't wasted time. If you take time out from activities, even for fifteen minutes, you allow yourself to reflect on your life, generate new ideas, and appreciate what's going on around you. It's why people take vacations and have days off. Slow time may not seem good for your schedule, but it's essential for you to learn.

Time It Right

As creatures originally designed to get food during the day and hide from predators at night, we're now free to work all day, all night or around the clock. If we work in tune with our bodies, we feel well. When we fight our cycles, we pay a price.

—Carol Orlock

As there is a pace to your thinking and a pattern to your sleep, your body has a natural rhythm for when it prefers to learn different types of things.

This was dubbed, by a former student of mine, "The Brains-Hands-Butt Model" for learning at the right time.

After poring over every bit of research I could get my hands on related to body cycles, energy cycles, learning, and attention (being careful to take regular breaks and follow the researchers' suggestions as best I could, to test their merit), I came up with this simple model to describe how your body learns best during the day.

Brain Time. First thing in the morning, when memories come easiest and your senses are most alert, when you're most likely to successfully grasp new concepts and understand technical or complicated details. Even though you think and remember with your whole body, your brain engages best between about 8:30 A.M. and 11:00 A.M. During this period, most people are also more willing to listen to you and learn with you, so this is the best time for technical classes, listening to a lecture, or meetings where you have lots of heavy information to convey. Use this time to take in through your senses, your eyes, and your ears all that you can.

Hands Time. In the middle of the day, after your body processes a meal, you're physically the strongest and the most flexible. From about 11:00 A.M. to 2:30 P.M., I encourage you to work with your hands, move things around, and use your strength and your adaptability. Spend this time being more active, taking information in through touch and movement, and synthesizing everything you can.

Butt Time. Then comes the afternoon lull, from about 2:30 P.M. to 6:00 P.M., when you're neither as quick to think nor as smooth in moving. This is the perfect time to rest on your sits bones, contemplate, and reflect. Even though you may feel like you're good for nothing, or too tired to learn any more, biologically, you're primed for reflection and rumination.

These three stages repeat their sequence during the night and early morning hours, which explains why you might feel alert and focused at 1:00 A.M. or sleep restlessly around 4:00 A.M. Consider using these guidelines to help you determine how to organize your day to get the most from what you want to learn.

Schedule Your Learning

Another dimension of timing your learning is to consider that your body operates a variety of activities in *ninety-minute cycles*. Although researchers initially discovered this while exploring sleep patterns, the same was found in situations ranging from problem-solving abilities, to hormone secretion, to sensitivity to tooth pain.

These cycles can also be subdivided into smaller fifteen-minute cycles. For example, most adults can focus on a specific concept or a routine for about forty-five minutes (three mini-cycles) before they need a break or another diversion to reenergize themselves.

If you have any control over your daily schedule, try to schedule what you do in ninety-minute, forty-five-minute, or even fifteen-minute cycles chunks.

Make a list of what you need to do, including time to reflect and ruminate, and then look at how these tasks might fit together with your body's preferred schedule.

Engage Your Pace

> The surest way to corrupt a youth is to instruct him to hold
> in higher esteem those who think alike than those who
> think differently.
>
> —*Friedrich Nietzsche*

In addition to using various paces to learn different things, we also have different internal speeds that reveal themselves as engagement styles. You might notice these styles if you work with people who are either quick or slow to talk about what they're thinking and learning. Just as some people are born to move faster or slower, some react quickly, and others speak up slowly.

The two engagement styles represent whether you talk to think or think to talk. If you *talk to think*, as you go along you talk about what you're doing and learning. If you *think to talk*, you keep your thoughts under wraps until you have something specific to say, or you understand how to proceed—or possibly until the learning experience is over.

Unfortunately, most formal learning events, including meetings and classes, do very little for either group: The talk-to-thinkers have little opportunity to speak, and the think-to-talkers rarely have enough time to reflect on what they're learning.

If you understand your style, you can be your own advocate to get what you need.

I saw the value of learning how people engage with each other while coaching a chief executive and his chief financial officer. I asked them both a simple question: "Do you talk to think or think to talk?" The CFO, a reserved accountant, thought about his answer, while his gregarious boss blurted out, "I talk." That one answer changed the nature of their working relationship. Prior to this conversation, it had never dawned on the CFO that the boss was just "thinking out loud" and said things simply to engage in conversation or to learn from the dialogue. And the CEO didn't understand why his most senior financial adviser hadn't challenged him more. From then on, whenever the CEO made a suggestion, the CFO took the opportunity to ask questions and learn how well his boss had thought out the plan. This improved their relationship and their company.

What's Your Style for Engaging?

Complete the following questionnaire to identify how you engage with information. Circle one of the two responses that characterizes your approach and add up the columns to find your score. Please answer as it applies to you right now. The column with the highest total represents your preferred engagement style.

I make decisions quickly.	I take time to reflect on my options.
I like a holistic approach.	I like a logical approach.
I take on several parts of a project at once.	I finish one thing before starting another.
I'm comfortable even when I'm uncertain of the conclusion.	I like to know there is a logical conclusion.
People say I'm quick to take action.	People say I'm slow to take action.
I don't need to know everything about a project before getting started.	I like to know the details before I start.

I'm quick to give an answer.

I like going point by point.

I tend to start projects without too much planning.

I tend to keep everything organized in an orderly fashion.

Total Talk to Think _____7_____

Total Think to Talk _____11_____

My engagement style: _____Talk to Think_____

If you are a talk-to-think learner, you will likely talk while learning. You might like to sound out ideas and say what's on your mind. Because you rely on other people's responses, you may prefer to work in a group or on a team. Sometimes you might hear yourself talking over people's conversations if they speak slowly or you may find yourself filling in the gaps between their comments.

If you're a think-to-talk learner, you probably wouldn't dare say something before you've thought it well through. You might need some additional quiet time to formulate a response to what you've heard. You may prefer to work alone or in a pair and might want to take your time when facing a challenging situation. You may find it tough to work in noisy environments with other activities going on.

Are You a Talk-to-Think Learner?

"Work? The time has come," the Walrus said,
"To talk of many things: Of shoes, and ships,
and sealing-wax, of cabbages, and kings."

—*Lewis Carroll*

If you're a talk-to-think learner, you tend to be quick in your decisions. When you face a complicated situation, you often jump right into the middle without much reflection. This can lead you to pick your approach with little thought about the consequences. From childhood, you may recall school days when you responded to your teacher's request by raising your hand quickly or just blurting out answers. Even now, your patience probably wears thin when you work with people who prefer to take their time before responding.

Tips for Talk-to-Think Learners

These tips will help you learn if you have a talk-to-think learning style. Discuss your favorites with another talk-to-think learner and then with a person who is a think-to-talk learner to discover how their approaches differ.

Be transparent. Introduce statements with, "I'm just thinking out loud here," and ask other people to point out when you're talking too much.

Announce your intentions. If you tend to talk a lot, people might not realize when you're actually ready to move forward. Let them know when you've reached a conclusion versus when you're just tossing ideas around.

Ask for comments. If you don't receive an opinion or a suggestion right away, be more specific in what you're asking for. Some people need time to absorb what you've asked before they can reply, and your clear request might help them to respond sooner.

Wait for a response. If you're prone to spit out ideas faster than the people around you can, first count to ten before offering your views. You might be surprised to hear someone else offer an idea you were thinking of—and may be relieved to know that other people are thinking the same thing.

Make Time to Think

If you're a talk-to-think learner, who works with other people in a group, you might have a tendency to jump into taking action on plans that the group hasn't fully explored. Next time, work with the group to make a list of the pros and the cons before making a decision.

+	−

Are You a Think-to-Talk Learner?

Do not the most moving moments of our lives
find us all without words?

—*Marcel Marceau*

If you're a think-to-talk learner, you probably prefer to take your time when you face a challenging situation. You've learned that you make better decisions when you can reflect on all the aspects of the problem.

To others, though, it may look like you're not participating because you're being quiet. Remind people that you are willing to offer your well-developed thoughts once you have had time to think through what's been said. The quality of your contribution improves when you have enough time to reflect. Note, however, that if you don't speak up or if you take too long to process and analyze a situation, you may lose your chance to have any say at all.

Tips for Think-to-Talk Learners

These tips will help you learn more if you have a think-to-talk learning style. Think about and then discuss your favorite tips with another think-to-talk learner and then with a talk-to-think learner to observe how their approaches differ.

Request more time. Ask for the amount of time you need to think everything through. Explain to people that if you have enough time, you will have a higher-quality response. "Could you give me a minute to think through this?" may create the necessary pause in a group activity for everyone to improve what they say.

Ask for help. When it's important to make a decision faster than you're comfortable with, ask for input from other people. Identify the less important parts of a decision first and then build toward making a final decision.

Practice sharing your thoughts. Verbalize your thoughts to a trusted friend—not so that this person can scrutinize you, but to practice sharing your ideas. With some rehearsal you can use your think-to-talk style to help other people to learn more.

Make Time to Analyze

If you're a think-to-talk learner who has to work with other people in a group, you might find it challenging to keep up with the pace of the conversation. Focus your energy, instead, on making a list of the pros and cons of any decisions under consideration so that you can share what you've thought about with the group. By tracking your thoughts, you can help the group make progress and make a wise choice.

+	−

10

Optimize Your Environment

We came into the world instinctively prepared to do two
things. One was to suck nourishment from our mother's
breasts. To accomplish this we used our sucking instinct.
The other was to do everything else. To accomplish this we
used our learning instinct.

—Peter Kline

Does the aroma of mint help you focus? Does Bonnie Raitt's music shift your thoughts into gear? Can you barely keep your eyes open after a big lunch? Do you feel relaxed near a sunny window?

A trigger activates each of your on-board learning systems. When you attempt to learn in an environment that optimizes those triggers, you're more apt to succeed. For example, some of us prefer absolute quiet, while other people find that background noise helps them think. Your environment influences your ability to learn more now.

This chapter introduces you to the various factors and triggers (both internal and external) that can help you create an optimal learning backdrop. It also explains how to compensate when it's time to learn and you have little control over the conditions around you. It addresses environmental elements and biological preferences that determine your ability to concentrate, focus, and learn. The more you can pay attention to your surroundings at the outset of learning something new, the more you can focus on the subject over time. As you learn how to modify your environment, you can also create optimal conditions for other types of work and for the time you spend learning at home and in your community.

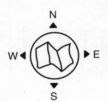

Road Map to This Chapter

Chapter 10 takes you to the following destinations:

▶ Creating the right space and seating

▶ Lighting and warming your environment

▶ Making your surroundings sound right

▶ Adding nature, beauty, and grace

▶ Eating and snacking on the right foods

Place and Space

> What, a university in the city? Why, the city is the university.
>
> —*Aristotle*

Where you learn can influence your ability to focus. Even if you can't rid yourself of the pressure and stresses in your life, you can adjust your environment in order to concentrate and learn more effectively. When you understand your unique physical needs, you can improve your ability to concentrate and stay alert.

Your task is to identify the locations and the conditions that suit your preferences and styles. Begin by asking yourself, "Where do I prefer to learn?" This might be one location or different places for learning various types of information. For example, do you picture an office, a parklike setting, your family room, a library, or a deserted beach? By recalling your favorite spots and some of their qualities, you can decide which conditions you might want to create when you try to learn something new. Take a moment now to reflect on the places and spaces where you have enjoyed learning.

Seating Preferences

> I played first chair in the high school band until they gave me an instrument.
>
> —*George R. Hext*

One environmental condition is the type of seat you prefer when you learn. Do you drop yourself down on the sofa, sit at a picnic table outside, or maybe find the cafeteria particularly helpful? For some people, a toilet gives them the structure (and the quiet surroundings) they need; for others, lying in bed provides the safety they enjoy.

Consider Darin, a sales manager and father of six, who finds that he learns best while sitting in a big comfortable chair in his family room, with his tablet computer on his lap. In this chair he doesn't worry about his feet hanging over the armrest, one of his daughters wanting to cuddle up beside him, or having an urge to turn himself upside down. He's always at ease.

In contrast, Debbie, a retired banker, knows that unless she's at a table, with her feet on the ground, her arms in front of her, and some structure to her environment, the sensations of the space around her become distracting and she finds herself trying to sit up even more straight.

First determine whether you prefer sitting in a traditional posture or in a more reclined position. Imagine an office chair, rather than a couch, a reclining chair, or a carpeted floor.

Then ask yourself: Is my best learning done on a soft or a hard surface? On comfortable furniture or on something sturdy and supportive? With my feet up or firmly planted on the floor?

If you're unsure which you prefer, spend some time trying different seating surfaces over the next few weeks to determine which work best for you.

If you prefer a soft chair, sit on a comfortable couch, an inflated exercise ball, or even a beanbag chair. If you prefer a sturdier seat, select a stool or a hardwood chair that keeps your back straight and your feet on the ground.

When you're required to use the equipment, the chairs, and the furniture that's available, remember that you can usually find ways to customize your space. For instance, if you prefer a more reclined or relaxed seat:

▶ Place a cushion or a pillow on your chair.

▶ Put your feet up, even if only on the leg supports of a table in front of you.

▶ Avoid chairs altogether and stand or sit on the floor.

No matter what your seating preference, keep some materials out of reach. If they are a few steps away, you'll need to stand up to get them and the short break will help to adjust your whole-body learning, which keeps your energy flowing.

Lighting Preference

> Darkness cannot drive out darkness; only light can do that.
>
> —*Martin Luther King, Jr.*

Another environmental condition is the amount and the type of light you prefer when you learn. Two home schooling moms I know have very different approaches to lighting.

Leanne finds that she prefers learning in a room without much light, where she can see only what she's working on, and everything around her fades from her attention. When she was young, her mother always told her to turn on the lights or it would harm her eyes, but she learned to use only enough light to see well and support her vision. The light is focused on what she's doing and on nothing else. Every once in a while she catches herself wanting to repeat her mother's words to her children, but then she realizes that they also prefer a dimly lit space.

Lisa, in contrast, turns on every lamp around her, pulls open the drapes, and soaks up the light. She feels weighed down by dark spaces; they drain her of the energy that light provides. She works outside with her children whenever she can, reading on her porch or working in the yard, and is always drawn to the brightest spot in any area.

Ask yourself: Are bright lights distracting or do they help me to see more clearly? Do I find that sunlight is comforting or has too much glare? Do I turn off most of the lights when I try to read or focus, or do I turn on lights to brighten up the space? Do any kinds of lights really bother me? Your answers will help you identify your lighting preferences.

I've met many people who find that they're sensitive to fluorescent lights—especially on a dreary day. Because so many schools and offices use fluorescent fixtures, you might not have a choice about working around them. Consider adding a lamp with a natural bulb in your immediate area.

If you prefer *dim light*, bright light might make you nervous, distract you, or sap your energy. As much as possible, keep the lights low around you. If you can't adjust the light, maybe you can diffuse it. Consider wearing a hat or sunglasses to prevent light from directly reaching your eyes. Soften the bright reflection on a page by covering it with a lightly colored transparency. Turn down the lights, sit away from windows, or install blinds.

If you prefer *bright light*, soft lighting might make you sluggish and sleepy. Add a desk lamp to your work area and point the lamp so that it shines directly on your material. Open the window shades, turn on the lights, and consider wearing light-colored clothes, or decorating with bright colors.

Temperature Preferences

> It doesn't matter what temperature the room is, it's always room temperature.
>
> —*Steven Wright*

In many offices and homes, people squabble over the thermostat. At meals and meetings, some people add on layers of clothing and others fan themselves to keep cool. Clearly, people have different internal temperature settings, and this has an effect on how they learn.

What level of temperature do you prefer while involved in learning activities? Ask yourself, Do I pile on layers of clothes until I'm warm, or do I lower the heat until I'm cool?

If you prefer to learn in an environment that's warm, you probably find that you accomplish less when the environment is cold. It seems like your energy is taking care of your physical needs first.

If you prefer staying warm:

► Keep a sweater or a jacket handy.

► Keep a pair of gloves or heavy socks nearby.

► Wear a long-sleeved shirt or blouse.

► Wear clothing made of material that holds warmth.

► Ask to borrow a sweater or a jacket when you're without one in a meeting.

► Keep a space heater in your immediate work or study area.

► Sit near a heating vent.

► Sit toward the center of the room, away from the windows and doors.

If you prefer to learn in cool environments, you're probably more productive when the temperature is low. When you're in an environment that's too warm, you might feel distracted and that you're accomplishing less.

If you prefer to keep cool:

► Sit near a barely opened window in the winter.

► Dress in layers so that you can adjust your clothing according to the temperature of the room.

▶ Evaluate the lighting to determine how much heat is being emitted; then decide whether it would help to turn the lights down or off.

▶ Wear clothing that breathes.

Brighten Your Senses

Now we will count to twelve
and we will all keep still
for once on the face of the earth,
let's not speak in any language;
let's stop for a second,
and not move our arms so much.

—Pablo Neruda

No matter whether you prefer bright light or dim, cool spaces or warm, sometimes, especially in the morning or late at night, you might find that your senses aren't as awake and alert as you'd like.

These exercises can help you warm up your senses so they can help you learn. Following a simple version of acupressure, which has been practiced for thousands of years, these exercises stimulate certain points for better thinking, seeing, and hearing.

Thinking

1. Whenever you feel under pressure or overwhelmed, put your fingertips on your forehead, above your eyebrows.

2. Keep them there while you think through your situation or talk it out.

3. Continue to hold your forehead lightly with your fingertips and tug up slightly.

4. Think through any leftover stressors, and then visualize pushing those thoughts out of the top of your head.

Hearing

Make sounds brighter and clearer and your attention sharper by giving your earlobes and ear edges a gentle massage. By doing this, you press several acupressure points, stimulating your whole body for a fast hearing boost.

Seeing

1. Sit upright in your chair. Without moving your head, look as far to the left as you can and hold your gaze for one full breath. Repeat, looking far to the right, and then up and down, holding each position in turn. Now move your eyes diagonally, from the upper right to the lower left, and then the upper left to the lower right. Repeat each diagonal move five times. Next, circle your eyes slowly several times, as if you were following the numbers on a clock, and then counterclockwise several times, keeping your head still.

2. Hold your right or left arm out in front of you, with your elbow bent and your thumb about a foot from your face. Shift your vision ten times back and forth between your thumb and the wall behind it.

3. For this exercise, if you wear glasses, take them off; contact lenses are okay. Begin by rubbing your palms together vigorously until they feel warm. With your fingers pointing up, gently cup your hands over your closed eyes. Don't press on your eyelids or rub your eyes. Imagine that you're seeing black. Feel the warmth from your palms relaxing the muscles around your eyes. Hold for one minute. Gently open your eyes and look around. You'll probably notice that colors seem brighter and that everything seems sharper and more defined.

Sound Preferences

> There are sounds to seasons. There are sounds to places.
> And there are sounds to every time in one's life.
>
> —*Alison Wyrley Birch*

To what extent do you prefer silence or background sounds while you concentrate or study? Maybe you wonder how your daughter can listen to music while doing her homework; meanwhile, you need either complete silence or, at most, classical music without words while you try to read. That's probably because you and your daughter have different sound preferences when you learn.

Each of us listens to the environment around us differently and hears something different, whether the moment-to-moment sounds, the flow of one musical phrase to the next, or how different noises work together or distract us from other sounds we hear.

> Ask yourself whether noise drives you nuts or whether quiet gives you the creeps.

> To learn, do I choose a place where it's quiet, or do I frequently work with the radio or the television on?

> Do sounds bother me when I study? Or, when there's no sound, am I actually more distracted than when there's a small amount of noise?

Some people strongly prefer a quiet place to concentrate. If you share this style, you may be extremely sensitive to any sound. You might hear fluorescent lights humming, water dripping in a far-off room, and computers buzzing when you're trying to focus. Equally distracting are people talking around you, loud noises, or the radio playing. Because you find it difficult to block out background sounds, you may find that your stress level goes up.

▶ When you're in an area with too many distracting noises, try to move someplace else.

▶ Use headphones to block out annoying sounds.

▶ Work in an empty room.

▶ Arrive earlier or stay later at work. Get up early or stay up late at home.

If you prefer background sounds when you learn, you have the ability to block out noise to the point where you don't really hear it or pay attention to it. Quiet can even create an emptiness that's distracting and uncomfortable.

▶ Listen to music and maybe even sing along.

▶ Turn on the television or radio, preferably to a show where people are talking.

▶ When people are learning around you, use headphones so that you don't disturb them.

▶ Work outside or open a window.

▶ Hum to yourself.

Learn with Music

Although many people prefer to learn in silence, mounting evidence suggests that some types of music help everyone read and remember. If you haven't found music helpful in the past, maybe you haven't tried a form of music that's compatible with the way you learn. The *ideal* music for learning has a slow, relaxing tempo of one beat per second. Mozart-type tunes are not the only ones that will work—any kind of music can relax and energize you. When you listen to something you enjoy, your energy levels rise and so does your ability to do good work.

If you're unsure whether music can help you, use this exercise to determine whether music aids your concentration and ability to memorize.

1. Try memorizing a random list of fifteen numbers while listening to a slow movement by a composer such as Handel, Bach, or Vivaldi.

2. Then try to memorize another list of fifteen numbers in silence.

3. Compare your success in both trials.

This experiment is only a rough gauge because many other factors influence how much you can recall accurately. Yet you may be pleasantly surprised to find that music apparently strengthens your ability to learn and remember.

Learn from Silence

Although many people prefer some noise when they learn, too much noise from cars, airplanes, and construction can lessen everyone's ability to learn from what we hear. Loud and jarring sounds from television, radio, children's toys, and even birds in the yard can diminish your ability to listen.

Counteract this by creating an environment where you can direct the degree of noise around you.

First, pause for a minute to take a deep breath while you listen to the sounds around you. Then, listen to the loudest noises, such as people talking, or a lawn mower.

Next, try listening to the sounds beneath the obvious noises, such as leaves rustling in the trees, clocks ticking on the wall, or footsteps tapping down the hall. Keep listening, layer by layer, until you hear your own breath and the beating of your heart.

Continue this exercise at least once a week by trying to listen for the spaces between sounds. Focus on the gaps in conversations, the pauses in music, and the absence of any sound between your breaths.

Make silence the theme for at least one day a month. If possible, immerse yourself in nature's sounds by spending the day walking in the woods, hiking in the mountains, or strolling along a beach. When you return, you'll feel refreshed and better able to listen.

Add Beauty

Grace is a simple quality that can be easily and inexpensively incorporated into your life.

—*Melinda Lee*

There are more elements to the environment around you than chairs, sounds, and temperatures. Two elements usually overlooked are beauty and the small graces that appear in nature but are often left out of indoor spaces. If you have looked around most offices or schools recently, you've probably noticed that they're designed for utility, rather than for learning.

I've found that an atmosphere that inspires awe helps me feel more at ease and interested in learning. Whenever you can, surround yourself with beauty.

Try adding something beautiful to your learning area. Use a vase of fresh flowers, a deep-green plant in a lovely pot, an impressionist painting in an interesting frame, an inspiring quotation written in a luxurious font, a memento from the past that reminds you of a fabulous day, or bright colors in an otherwise dreary room. Listen to nature sounds, or open your blinds so that you can see the outdoors.

After you've made a change, reflect on what happened. I suspect you found that having beauty nearby lifted your spirit and influenced your state of mind. That's because we pick up knowledge from aspects of our surroundings that we may not even notice. Like good food, exercise, deep rest, and physical connection, beauty is a fundamental nutrient that ought to be included in our daily diet.

Clear Your Space

> How can we communicate the importance of opening
> spaces in the imagination where persons can reach beyond
> where they are?
>
> —*Maxine Greene*

Sometimes, I find that to create a little space to learn in my life, I need to clear my physical space. Take a moment to look around you. What have you kept that you don't use, need, like, or even want anymore? Clear your space of possessions that no longer serve a useful purpose. Donate. Recycle. Give things away. Throw them in the trash. When you clear out your space, other perspectives, experiences, and lessons can come into your life.

Scent Sense

> First I ripen, then I rot.
>
> —*Woody Allen*

There are also internal elements that influence our environment and how we learn.

One day when I had a hard time concentrating, I decided to clean out a drawer. All of a sudden, I had a strong sense that my mind was now clear and I could get back to my reading. This happened just as I held a candle in a tin that had been given to me as a gift. I opened the tin and inhaled the candle's strong scent of vanilla and mint. That day I focused so well that, for the rest of the project, I opened the tin daily before starting my work.

This happened because certain scents affect brain activity, our sense of alertness, and even our mood. The candle's mint and vanilla scents both help with concentration and focus, and therefore learning.

Lemon balm *(Melissa officinalis)* also has a focusing and soothing effect that can help you learn. Oils that give lemon balm its citrusy scent calm your nervous system and help you filter out excessive stimuli from your environment.

Other learning-friendly scents include rosemary, thyme, lavender, sandalwood, and sweet basil. You can invoke their help with a scented candle near your learning space or a hand lotion that leaves a scent on your skin. Spend a moment thinking about which scents help you focus.

Learner-Friendly Foods and Drinks

> One cannot think well, love well, sleep well, if one has not dined well.
>
> *—Virginia Woolf*

Finally, take into account the environment you create *inside yourself* by the foods and beverages you consume. I want to send you off with practical ideas that you can easily use to change your menu and the snacks you choose, which will transform your alertness and your ability to learn.

Basic Ingredients for Learning

Five basic ingredients can keep your whole body in peak condition and enhance your learning throughout the day.

Water
Protein-rich foods
Fats
Complex carbohydrates
Vitamins and minerals

Ingredient 1: Water

More than half of your body is made up of water, and when you're even slightly dehydrated, the unnecessary stress can prevent the kind of thinking that's required to learn.

Do you have some water nearby right now? Water is so important for learning that if you don't have a glass of water at hand, I encourage you to stop reading and get one now. Sip it slowly while you continue to read. Make a habit of filling a water glass or a jug in the morning, and continue to sip and refill it throughout the day.

If you don't particularly like the way water tastes, modify the flavor a little. For instance, I prefer my water with a slice of lemon (or lime) or a quick dunk from a peppermint tea bag to add a little zing.

How much water does your body need? Here's a quick test: Divide your body weight by two. If you weigh 150 pounds, half your weight would be 75 pounds. Your body requires that you take in an ounce of water every day for each of those pounds. In this example, you should drink 75 ounces of water daily. If you're wondering why the "eight glasses of water rule" so many of us grew up with doesn't always apply, that's because it was probably based on a person who weighs 128 pounds.

If you're serious about learning, I encourage you to make water your beverage of choice and drink up.

Ingredient 2: Protein-Rich Foods

Another important ingredient at each meal is protein-rich foods. They form the foundation for learning-friendly nutrition because they contain amino acids that help you stay alert. Foods rich in protein include fish, seafood, eggs, meat, poultry, nuts, beans, peas, lentils, cheese, yogurt, and many soy products. When these foods break down into their base molecules, your body more effectively creates three neurotransmitters—serotonin, dopamine, and norepinephrine—commonly associated with memory and your ability to learn.

Ingredient 3: Fats

The next ingredient to consider is fat. Many people believe that all fats are unhealthy, but some fats are essential for your body to function properly. After all, 60 percent of your brain is made up of fat. A deficiency of fat in your diet can diminish your ability to function.

Essential fatty acids help to form myelin coatings around your nerves that help your neural pathways. If this coating breaks down as a result of too little essential fatty acid in your diet, you would find that your nerve impulses slow and you'd have trouble with your focus and memory.

One of the most important essential fatty acids is omega-3, which provides a fluid your brain uses to carry messages from one cell to another. You'll find omega-3 in oily fish—for example, salmon, trout, sardines, and mackerel—as well as in flax seeds, pumpkin seeds, soy nuts, and walnuts.

Ingredient 4: Complex Carbohydrates

A small amount of complex carbohydrates, from whole wheat bread, brown rice, or an apple, provides an excellent source of glucose which is the most basic type of energy and the main fuel to help you learn. Even though all foods will eventually break down into glucose, carbohydrates reach this stage faster than protein does. I caution you not to consume too many carbohydrates while you try to learn, however, because they also create serotonin, which sends the body a signal to relax, feel calm, and get sleepy.

Ingredient 5: Vitamins and Minerals

Vitamins and minerals offer fine-tuning for your whole body. You could obtain them from specially enhanced drinks or supplements, but your body absorbs nutrients from foods more efficiently. You will also find that "smart drinks" and heavily supplemented blends are expensive and not nearly as enjoyable as a nutritious meal.

Ingredients to Skip

What you don't eat and drink is just as important in enhancing your learning as what you do eat. Here are some things to avoid.

Alcohol. If you're tempted to have a drink when you need to concentrate, think carefully about your choice of beverage. Alcohol depresses brain function, slows the speed of learning, and makes it more difficult to pay attention.

Caffeine. For alertness, a little coffee, caffeinated tea, or cola soda pop can give you a quick lift, but too much can backfire. The caffeine in coffee energizes you, but because it's a stimulant, it can also keep you up at night and can overwhelm your system if you drink too much. Caffeine also dehydrates your body, eventually leaving it more tired than it was before.

Two alternatives are *yerba maté*, a traditional South American drink, and green tea, which has less caffeine than decaffeinated coffee, but has a stimulating effect. You can buy both at most supermarkets and health food stores.

Sugar. Although you can get a quick lift from sugar or sugary foods, over time they can leave you less energetic than when you started. Sugar goes straight to your bloodstream, giving you an energy boost, but, unfortunately, the effect won't last. Your body counters with massive amounts of insulin to help process the sugar, and soon your energy level is lower than before.

Simple carbohydrates. Pasta, starchy vegetables, breads, cereals, and bananas spike your blood sugar level and then it drops, making you sleepy. These foods are much better suited to an evening meal, which is usually a time when you want to relax.

Overeating. If you eat too much, even of foods that promote alertness, you'll feel uninterested in doing anything other than sleep. Think of your body as a factory with several production lines: When the food-processing line has too much coming through, it needs to take workers from other areas to deal with the amount of food you've eaten. As a result, your learning capacity diminishes while you digest all of that food.

What's Your Snack Style?

> Fear less, hope more; eat less, chew more; whine less,
> breathe more; talk less, say more; hate less, love more, and
> all good things are yours.
>
> —*Swedish proverb*

In addition to eating a healthy meal, you might find that snacking helps you to concentrate. Some people, however, get distracted if they eat when trying to learn and find their attention on the snack, not on their work.

If you stay focused longer if you eat while you read and chew gum when you listen to other people, snacking helps you stay focused by creating rhythm, physical movement, and added energy. When food isn't readily available, you might find yourself chewing on a pencil, a pen cap, or a paper clip. If you feel mentally stuck, a snack can help you refocus your energy. The physical action of your moving jaw helps you learn.

Some snacks are more learning-friendly than others. If you're a snacker, set out a bowl containing almonds, walnuts, soy nuts, pumpkin seeds, or sesame seeds as an ideal alternative to sugary snacks.

If these snacks don't offer the crunch or the variety you crave, try small pretzels, baby carrots, popcorn, turkey jerky, dried apples, celery sticks, hard-boiled eggs, or low-fat cheese.

No matter which snacks you prefer, put your snack in a dish, rather than eating it straight out of a bag or a box. That way, you can monitor exactly how much and how quickly you eat.

Another alternative is to chew gum. Research shows that chewing gum may improve your memory by up to 35 percent. The key is the repetitive chewing motion. People recalled more words and performed better on short-term memory tests after concentrating while they chewed gum. Their internal environment improved their learning potential.

Bravo!

Finish each day and be done with it. You have
done what you could. Some blunders and
absurdities no doubt crept in; forget them as
soon as you can. Tomorrow is a new day; begin
it well and serenely and with too high a spirit to
be encumbered with your old nonsense.
—*Ralph Waldo Emerson*

Congratulations. You have come a long way. The fact that you read this
book makes a strong statement that you're serious about growing,
changing, and learning. If you consider what I wrote and use this information to take charge of your learning, I know from experience that you'll
greatly enhance your chances to learn more.

Always remember that you learn easily when you use strategies to match
your personal styles. Nevertheless, if you were to label yourself *only* a visual
learner or a person who is learner-motivated, you'll have missed an opportunity to reach new heights and develop new skills.

Become aware of your preferences and use them. You'll find learning
easier and faster than ever before. Extend your pathways and perspectives so
that you can build a wide range of learning techniques. When you do, you'll
have equipped yourself for learning and success. You will be able to learn
more now.

Recommended Resources

I f you're interested in learning more from the materials in this book, you'll find ample resources in this section. My personal web site (www.marciaconner.com) contains even more resources, along with reviews and the citations for the scientific information in the book.

General Learning Resources

The resources listed here offer supplemental information for any of the chapters in this book and are useful for deepening or broadening your knowledge on how people learn.

Adult Learner: The Definitive Classic in Adult Education and Human Resource Development, 5th ed. Malcolm S. Knowles. Houston, Texas: Gulf Publishing, 1998.

How People Learn: Brain, Mind, Experience, and School. John D. Bransford, M. Suzanne Donovan, and James W. Pellegrino, eds. Washington: D.C.: National Academy Press, 2000.

Human Learning, 3rd ed. Jeanne Ellis Ormrod. Upper Saddle River, N.J.: Prentice-Hall, 1999.

Ageless Learner (www.agelesslearner.com) has a comprehensive web site focused on how learning and curiosity influence everything you do in life, no matter your age. It offers resources and information to help you get more out of life whether you're four years old or ninety-four.

The Learnativity Alliance (www.learnativity.org) is a non-profit organization dedicated to the notion that individual and organizational effectiveness depends on learning better, faster, smarter, and through the consistent application of learning, combined with creativity, flexibility, and paying close attention to the right things.

Learning in the New Economy magazine (www.linezine.com) is an editorially independent online publication introducing the best thinking on learning, performance, knowledge, and human capital.

Performance Concepts International (PCI) provides excellent assessments, surveys, and customized training to individual learners, teams, and leaders. Learn more online (www.pcilearn.com) or by calling founder Susan Rundle at (203) 743-5743.

General Resources for Working with Young Learners

All That You Are. Woodleigh Marx Hubbard. New York: Putnam, 2000. Beautifully illustrated book written for boys and girls 4 to 8 years old.

Discover Your Child's Learning Style: Children Learn in Unique Ways. Mariaemma Willis and Victoria Kindle-Hodson. Rocklin, Calif.: Prima Publishing, 1999.

A Mind at a Time. Mel Levine. New York: Simon and Schuster, 2002. This book helps parents recognize and teach to their child's intellectual, emotional, and physical strengths.

When I Grow Up I Want to Be Me. Sandra Magsamen. New York: Orchard Books, 2002. Written specifically for 4- to 8-year-old girls.

Free Spirit Publishing (www.freespirit.com) offers books designed to support young people and promote positive self-esteem through improved social and learning skills.

Chapter 1: Find Your Motivation

Coloring Outside the Lines. Roger C. Schank. New York: Quill, 2001.

The Courage to Teach: Exploring the Inner Landscape of a Teacher's Life. Parker J. Palmer. San Francisco: Jossey-Bass, 1997.

First Things First: To Live, to Love, to Learn, to Leave a Legacy. Stephen R. Covey, A. Roger Merrill, and Rebecca R. Merrill. New York: Fireside, 1996.

Homework Without Tears: A Parent's Guide for Motivating Children to Do Homework and to Succeed in School. Lee Canter. New York: HarperCollins, 1993.

The Inquiring Mind: A Study of the Adult Who Continues to Learn, 3rd ed. Cyril O. Houle. Madison, Wisc.: University of Wisconsin Press, 1993.

Learning All the Time. John Holt. Cambridge, Mass.: Perseus; reprint, 1990.

Lifebalance: How to Simplify and Bring Harmony to Everyday Life. Linda Eyre and Richard Eyre. New York: Fireside, 1997.

Punished by Rewards: The Trouble with Gold Stars, Incentive Plans, A's, Praise, and Other Bribes. Alfie Kohn. Boston: Houghton Mifflin, 1999.

Teach Your Own: The John Holt Book of Homeschooling. John Holt and Patrick Farenga. Cambridge, Mass.: Perseus, 2003.

The About web site (www.adulted.about.com) offers a section on education for people of all ages and an especially thorough section on adult continuing education that contains links and reviews of materials related to all facets of learning in adulthood, including reviews and links to sites you can visit to enroll in courses.

AskERIC (ericir.syr.edu/) offers a clearinghouse and online database of over 3,000 articles, online books, Internet sites, educational organizations, and electronic discussion groups on all aspects of education for people of all ages.

How Difficult Can This Be? The F.A.T. City Workshop, 1989. This powerful video helps you understand the frustration, anxiety, and tension that people who have learning disabilities face each day. You can order this compelling video online (www.ricklavoie.com/videos.html) or by calling LDOnline at (800) 343-5540.

Home Education Magazine (www.home-ed-magazine.com) is a terrific resource for parents who want to teach their children at home as their child's primary source of schooling or who want to help nurture a sense of ongoing learning with their children who attend a traditional school. The magazine is one offering from the American Homeschool Education Association [(www.nhen.com) National Home Education Network (NHEN)].

The Informal Education web site (www.infed.org) offers a wide array of learning-related resources.

We Blog: Publishing Online with Weblogs. Paul Bausch, Matthew Haughey, Meg Hourihan. John Wiley & Sons, 2002. Learn more online (www.blogger.com).

Marc J. Rosenberg (www.marcrosenberg.com), the author of the book *e-Learning: Strategies for Delivering Knowledge in the Digital Age.* (New York: McGraw Hill, 2000), hosts a web site full of useful articles, presentations, and advice if you're interested in looking further into learning online.

Michigan State University, through its MSU Global Online Connection (www.msuglobal.com/), offers courses on a wide range of practical subjects, from container gardening to global community security, as well as a number of degree programs.

The Open Directory Project (www.dmoz.org/reference/education/) enlists people to read web sites, review them, and categorize them in order to make them easy to find and use. The web site has categories on learning how to learn, as well as many categories where you can find formal and informal educational opportunities on most any subject imaginable.

Chapter 2: Learn Your Nature

Accelerated Learning for the 21st Century: The Six-Step Plan to Unlock Your Master-Mind. Colin Penfield Rose and Malcolm J. Nicholl. New York: Dell, 1998.

Fundamentals of Graphic Language. David Sibbet. San Francisco: Grove Consultants International, 1993. Order online (www.grove.com) or call 800-49GROVE/415-561-2500.

The Gift of Dyslexia: Why Some of the Smartest People Can't Read and How They Can Learn. Ronald D. Davis. New York: Perigee, 1997.

How to Implement and Supervise a Learning Style Program. Rita Stafford Dunn. Alexandria, Va.: Association for Supervision and Curriculum Development, 1996.

How to Read a Book. Mortimer Adler and Charles Van Doren. New York: Simon and Schuster, 1972.

How to Speak, How to Listen. Mortimer Adler. New York: Collier Books, 1997.

How Your Child Is Smart: A Life-Changing Approach to Learning. Dawna Markova and Anne R. Powell. Emeryville, Calif.: Conari Press, 1992.

In the Mind's Eye: Visual Thinkers, Gifted People with Dyslexia and Other Learning Difficulties, Computer Images, and the Ironies of Creativity. Thomas G. West. Amherst, N.Y.: Prometheus, 1997.

Intelligence Reframed: Multiple Intelligences for the 21st Century. Howard Gardner. New York: Basic Books, 2000.

Listen and Learn. Cheri J. Meiners. Minneapolis, Minn.: Free Spirit Publishing, 2003. With simple words and inviting illustrations, this book introduces to four- to eight-year-olds what listening means, why it's important, how to listen well, and the positive results of being a good listener.

Mapping Inner Space: Learning and Teaching Mind Mapping, 2nd ed. Nancy Margulies. Tucson, Ariz.: Zephyr Press, 2001.

The Mind Map Book: How to Use Radiant Thinking to Maximize Your Brain's Untapped Potential. Tony Buzan. New York: Plume, 1996.

The New Drawing on the Right Side of the Brain, 2nd ed. Betty Edwards. New York: J. P. Tarcher, 1999.

A Picture's Worth 1,000 Words: A Workbook for Visual Communications. Jean Westcott. San Francisco: Jossey-Bass, 1996.

Please Understand Me: Character and Temperament Types, 5th ed. David Keirsey and Marilyn Bates. Del Mar, Calif.: Prometheus Nemesis, 1984.

Rapid Reading Made E-Z. Paul R. Scheele. Deerfield Beach, Fla.: Made E-Z Products, 2000.

An Unused Intelligence: Physical Thinking for 21st Century Leadership. Andy Bryner and Dawna Markova. Emeryville, Calif.: Conari Press, 1996.

Visual Explanations: Images and Quantities, Evidence and Narrative. Edward R. Tufte. Cheshire, Conn.: Graphics Press, 1997.

Who Are You? 101 Ways of Seeing Yourself. Malcolm Godwin. New York: Penguin, 2000.

Cook's Illustrated (www.cooksillustrated.com) provides visual instructions on how to cook almost anything. Books and a terrific magazine can be obtained through the web site.

Map your thoughts visually with Mindjet software (www.mindman.com) and the concept map software from Inspiration (www.inspiration.com).

The Multiple Intelligences for Adult Literacy and Education web site (www.literacyworks.org/mi/intro/) describes the theory of multiple intelligences and includes a terrific list of resources so you can learn more.

Zome System tools are available from their manufacturer (www.zometools.com) and from MindWare Online (www.mindwareonline.com)

Chapter 3: Engage Your Body

Ageless Body, Timeless Mind: The Quantum Alternative to Growing Old. Deepak Chopra. New York: Three Rivers Press, 1998.

Age Power: How the 21st Century Will Be Ruled by the New Old. Ken Dychtwald. New York: J. P. Tarcher, 1999. Also see Ken Dychtwald's web site (www.agewave.com).

Age Wave: How the Most Important Trend of Our Time Will Change Our Future. Ken Dychtwald. New York: Bantam Doubleday, 1990.

The Art of Growing Up: Simple Ways to Be Yourself at Last. Veronique Vienne. New York: Clarkson N. Potter, 2000.

The Biology of Transcendence: A Blueprint of the Human Spirit. Joseph Chilton Pearce. Rochester, Vt.: Inner Traditions, 2002.

Bodymind. Ken Dychtwald. New York: Random House, 1977.

Body, Mind, and Sport: The Mind-Body Guide to Lifelong Health, Fitness, and Your Personal Best. John Douillard. New York: Three Rivers Press, 2001.

Brain Gym: Simple Activities for Whole Brain Learning. Paul E. Dennison and Gail E. Dennison. Glendale, Calif.: Edu-Kinesthetics, 1992.

Cycles: How We Will Live, Work, and Buy. Maddy Dychtwald. New York: The Free Press, 2003.

Descartes' Error: Emotion, Reason, and the Human Brain. Antonio R. Damasio. New York: Avon Books, 1995.

Desktop Yoga: The Anytime, Anywhere Relaxation Program for Office Slaves, Internet Addicts, and Stressed-Out Students. Julie T. Lusk. New York: Perigee, 1998.

The Emotional Brain: The Mysterious Underpinnings of Emotional Life. Joseph Ledoux. New York: Touchstone Books, 1998.

Evolution's End: Claiming the Potential of Our Intelligence. Joseph Chilton Pearce. San Francisco: Harper, 1993.

Geeks and Geezers. Warren G. Bennis and Robert J. Thomas. Boston: Harvard Business School Press, 2002.

The Heart's Code: Tapping the Wisdom and Power of Our Heart Energy. Paul Pearsall. New York: Broadway Books, 1999.

How Brains Think: Evolving Intelligence, Then and Now. William H. Calvin. New York: Basic Books, 1997.

Inner Knowing: Consciousness, Creativity, Insight, and Intuition. Helen Palmer, ed. New York: J. P. Tarcher, 1999.

Inner Simplicity: 100 Ways to Regain Peace and Nourish Your Soul. Elaine St. James. New York: Hyperion, 1995.

Learn to Remember. Dominic O'Brien. San Francisco: Chronicle Books, 2000.

The Memory Bible: An Innovative Strategy for Keeping Your Brain Young. Gary Small. New York: Hyperion Books, 2002.

Mind over Matter: Personal Choices for a Lifetime of Fitness. Susan Cantwell. Toronto, Canada: Stoddart Publishing, 1999.

Molecules of Emotion: Why You Feel the Way You Feel. Candace B. Pert. New York: Simon and Schuster, 1997.

Never Too Late: My Musical Life Story. John Holt. Cambridge, Mass.: Perseus, 1991.

No Need for Speed: A Beginner's Guide to the Joy of Running. John Bingham. New York: Rodale Press, 2002.

Office Yoga: Simple Stretches for Busy People. Darrin Zeer. Illustrated by Michael Klein. San Francisco: Chronicle Books, 2000.

The Owner's Manual for the Brain: Everyday Applications from Mind-Brain Research, 2nd ed. Pierce J. Howard. Austin, Tex.: Bard Press, 2000.

Power Hunch. Marcia Emory. Hillsboro, Oreg.: Beyond Words Publishing, 2001.

Smart Moves: Why Learning Is Not All in Your Head. Carla Hannaford. Arlington, Va.: Great Ocean Publishing, 1995.

A User's Guide to the Brain: Perception, Attention, and the Four Theaters of the Brain. John J. Ratey. New York: Vintage Books, 2002.

Your Body Believes Every Word You Say: The Language of the Bodymind Connection, 2nd ed. Barbara Hoberman Levine. Fairfield, Conn.: WordsWork Press, 2000.

The AARP web site (www.aarp.org/learn/) offers terrific articles, practical information, and suggestions on how to learn most anything at age fifty-plus.

Brain, Child magazine (www.brainchildmag.com) is a quarterly publication for thinking moms that also serves as a community for and by mothers who like to think about what raising children does for and to the mind and soul.

The Dana Foundation (www.dana.org) web site serves as a gateway to general information about the brain and current brain research, sites related to more than twenty-five brain disorders, and Brainy Kids Online, which offers children, parents, and teachers resources on the brain for younger children.

Elderhostel (www.elderhostel.org) is a not-for-profit organization dedicated to providing extraordinary learning adventures for people age fifty-five and over.

The Learning Brain (www.learningbrain.com) is an outstanding monthly newsletter on the latest findings in brain research and learning.

The OASIS Institute (www.oasisnet.org) offers challenging education programs in the arts, humanities, wellness, and technology to enhance the quality of life for mature adults.

Shape Up America (www.shapeup.org) offers a sensible exercise and movement program based on taking 10,000 steps a day.

Chapter 4: Open New Pathways

The Art of Possibility: Transforming Professional and Personal Life. Rosamund Stone Zander and Benjamin Zander. Boston: Harvard Business School Press, 2000.

The Artist's Way: A Spiritual Path to Higher Creativity. Julia Cameron. New York: J. P. Tarcher, 2002.

Baby Minds: Brain-Building Games Your Baby Will Love. Linda Acredolo and Susan Goodwyn. New York: Bantam Doubleday, 2000.

Birth of the Chaordic Age. Dee Hock. San Francisco: Berrett-Koehler, 2000.

Breakaway: Deliver Value to Your Customers—Fast! Charles L. Fred. San Francisco: Jossey-Bass, 2002. Although this book appears to be all business, it's really about how people learn and master new information, and how approaching personal competencies can improve your working and business relationships with anyone.

Complexity: The Emerging Science at the Edge of Order and Chaos. Mitchell M. Waldrop. New York: Simon and Schuster, 1992.

Discover Your Genius: How to Think Like History's Ten Most Revolutionary Minds. Michael Gelb. New York: Quill, 2003.

How to Think Like Leonardo da Vinci: 7 Steps to Everyday Genius. Michael Gelb. New York: Dell Books, 2000.

Learning How to Learn: Psychology and Spirituality in the Sufi Way. Idries Shah. New York: Penguin, 1996.

Nobody in Charge: Essays on the Future of Leadership. Harlan Cleveland. San Francisco: Jossey-Bass, 2002.

Now, Discover Your Strengths. Marcus Buckingham and Donald Clifton. New York: Free Press, 2001.

The Path of Least Resistance: Learning to Become the Creative Force in Your Own Life. Robert Fritz. New York: Fawcett Books, 1989.

Peripheral Visions: Learning Along the Way. Mary Catherine Bateson. New York: Perennial, 1995.

Steps to an Ecology of Mind: Collected Essays in Anthropology, Psychiatry, Evolution, and Epistemology. Gregory Bateson and Mary Catherine Bateson. Chicago: University of Chicago Press, 2000.

To Know as We Are Known: Education as a Spiritual Journey. Parker J. Palmer. San Francisco: Harper, 1993.

Transformative Dimensions of Adult Learning. Jack Mezirow. San Francisco: Jossey-Bass, 1991.

Chapter 5: Attend and Observe

ADD-Friendly Ways to Organize Your Life. Judith Kolberg and Kathleen Nadeau. New York: Brunner-Routledge, 2002. This book deals with the problem of disorganization and how anyone can develop good organizing habits.

The Highly Sensitive Person: How to Thrive When the World Overwhelms You. Elaine N. Aron. New York: Broadway Books, 1997.

Journeys Through ADDulthood. Sari Solden. New York: Walker and Co., 2002.

Learning Outside the Lines. Jonathan Mooney and David Cole. New York: Fireside, 2000.

Memory and Attention: An Introduction to Human Information Processing. Donald A. Norman. New York: John Wiley and Sons, 1969.

More Balls Than Hands: Juggling Your Way to Success by Learning to Love Your Mistakes. Michael Gelb. Upper Saddle River, N.J.: Prentice-Hall, 2003.

The Power of Mindful Learning. Ellen J. Langer. Cambridge, Mass.: Perseus, 1998.

The Scent of Eros: Mysteries of Odor in Human Sexuality. James V. Kohl and Robert T. Francoeur. Lincoln, Neb.: iUniverse, 2002. This easy-to-read, scientifically supported book offers an incredible amount of information on human pheromones, covering their influence on all types of behavior and what this might mean for society.

Shadow Syndromes. John J. Ratey and Catherine Johnson. New York: Bantam Books, 1998.

Turn It Off: How to Unplug from the Anytime-Anywhere Office Without Disconnecting Your Career. Gil E. Gordon. New York: Three Rivers Press, 2001.

View from the Cliff: A Course in Achieving Daily Focus. Lynn Weiss. Dallas, Tex.: Taylor Publications, 2001.

Women with Attention Deficit Disorder: Embracing Disorganization at Home and in the Workplace. Sari Solden. Grass Valley, Calif.: Underwood Books, 2002.

You Mean I'm Not Lazy, Stupid or Crazy?! A Self-help Book for Adults with Attention Deficit Disorder. Kate Kelly and Peggy Rumundo. New York: Fireside, 1996.

Chapter 6: Mind Your Gaps

Crossing the Unknown Sea: Work as a Pilgrimage of Identity. David Whyte. New York: Riverhead Books, 2001.

The Knowing-Doing Gap: How Smart Companies Turn Knowledge into Action. Jeffrey Pfeffer and Robert I. Sutton. Boston: Harvard Business School Press, 2000.

The Knowledge Evolution: Expanding Organizational Intelligence. Verna Allee. Boston: Butterworth-Heinemann, 1997.

The Social Life of Information. John Seely Brown and Paul Duguid. Boston: Harvard Business School Press, 2000.

Spiritual Serendipity: Cultivating and Celebrating the Art of the Unexpected. Richard M. Eyre. New York: Simon and Schuster, 1997.

Chapter 7: Get Together

Beyond the Myths and Magic of Mentoring: How to Facilitate an Effective Mentoring Process. Margo Murray. New York: John Wiley & Sons, 2001.

Coaching for Performance: Growing People, Performance and Purpose, 3rd ed. John Whitmore. Sonoma, Calif.: Nicholas Brealey, 2002.

Communities of Practice: Learning, Meaning, and Identity. Etienne Wenger. Cambridge, England: Cambridge University Press, 1999. Also see the author's web site (www.cpsquare.com).

The Handbook of Coaching: A Comprehensive Resource Guide for Managers, Executives, Consultants, and HR. Frederic M. Hudson. San Francisco: Jossey-Bass, 1999.

In Good Company: How Social Capital Makes Organizations Work. Don Cohen and Laurence Prusak. Boston: Harvard Business School Press, 2001.

Organizing Genius: The Secrets of Creative Collaboration. Warren G. Bennis and Patricia Ward Biederman. Cambridge, Mass.: Perseus, 1998.

Take Time for Your Life: A Personal Coach's Seven-Step Program for Creating the Life You Want. Cheryl Richardson. New York: Broadway Books, 1999.

Turning to One Another: Simple Conversations to Restore Hope to the Future. Margaret J. Wheatley. San Francisco: Berrett-Koehler, 2002.

The Virtual Community: Homesteading on the Electronic Frontier. Revised edition. Howard Rheingold. Cambridge, Mass.: MIT Press, 2002.

The Bootstrap Alliance web site (www.bootstrapalliance.org) is full of research, discussion, and resources on how to improve the collective IQ of any organization.

Coach University and Corporate Coach University offer a variety of personal and corporate coach training programs along with courses for the general public, including "What's Coaching All About." For more information on these programs call (800)-48-COACH. (Online, visit www.coachu.com for the personal coaching program and www.cccui.com for the professional coaching program.)

Creating Learning Communities (www.creatinglearningcommunities.org) is an online book developed by the Coalition for Self-Learning.

The International Coach Federation (www.coachfederation.org) is the largest nonprofit professional organization of personal and business coaches that provides an online referral service.

Chapter 8: Jump In

Don't Just Do Something, Sit There: New Maxims to Refresh and Enrich Your Life. Richard Eyre. New York: Simon and Schuster, 1995.

Experience and Education. John Dewey. New York: Touchstone Books, 1997.

Failing Forward: How to Make the Most of Your Mistakes. John C. Maxwell. Nashville, Tenn.: Thomas Nelson, 2000.

The Fifth Discipline Field Book: Strategies and Tools for Building a Learning Organization. Peter M. Senge, Art Kleiner, Charlotte Roberts, Rick Ross, and Bryan Smith. New York: Doubleday, 1994.

A Year to Live: How to Live This Year as if It Were Your Last. Stephen Levine. New York: Bell Tower, 1977.

Chapter 9: Pace Yourself

The Art of the Long View: Paths to Strategic Insight for Yourself and Your Company. Peter Schwartz. New York: Doubleday, 1996.

Hare Brain, Tortoise Mind: How Intelligence Increases When You Think Less. Guy Claxton. New York: Perennial, 1999.

Inner Time: The Science of Body Clocks and What Makes Us Tick. Carol Orlock. Secaucus, N.J.: Birch Lane Press, 1993.

Time Shifting, Creating More Time for Your Life. Stephan Rechtschaffern. New York: Doubleday, 1997.

Chapter 10: Optimize Your Environment

The Biology of Success. Robert Arnot. New York: Little Brown, 2001.

The Chair: Rethinking Culture, Body, and Design. Galen Cranz. New York: W. W. Norton, 2000.

Clear Your Clutter with Feng Shui. Karen Kingston. New York: Broadway Books, 1999. This books helps you organize your life by teaching you how to sort out your junk and declutter your thoughts and your space.

Nurture Bear: The Treasure Hunt. Sarah Hendred and Claudie Phillips. Illustrated by Lauren M. Davies. Westmont, Ill.: Long Hill Productions, 2003. This book takes a child on a journey, teaching her how to identify healthy and nurturing food. Also visit the book's web site (www.shortmountains.com).

Sandra Leyland Williams's Natural Health web site (www.clicknutrition. co.uk) offers articles and resources on learning-friendly nutrition.

Index